Steiff TOYS
REVISITED

Steiff™ TOYS
REVISITED

JEAN WILSON

513-773-7701

Wallace-Homestead Book Company
Radnor, Pennsylvania

Designed by Anthony Jacobson
Manufactured in the United States of America

Library of Congress Cataloging in Publication Data
Wilson, Jean (Jean Baker)
    Steiff toys revisited / Jean Wilson.
      p. cm.
    ISBN 0-87069-538-X
    1. Margarete Steiff GmbH—Catalogs. 2. Teddy bears—Germany
(West)—Collectors and collecting—Catalogs. 3. Dolls—Germany
(West)—Collectors and collecting—Catalogs. I. Title.
NK9509.65.M37A4   1989
688.7'2'0943471—dc20   89-50514
                                                      CIP

1 2 3 4 5 6 7 8 9 0   8 7 6 5 4 3 2 1 0 9

Contents

Acknowledgments

Compiling this book was possible only with the help I received from many different sources. I would like to thank everyone who assisted me.

Shortly before the deadline for the book, I was saddened by the death of my friend Virginia Heitzman, of Piqua, Ohio, who painted the watercolor used on the cover using Margaret Strong bears as models. This book is dedicated to her memory.

The London office of Sotheby's has been most helpful by supplying many photos for the auction section. I would like to thank Bunny Campione of the Collectors' Department for her cooperation. Christie's of London also contributed photos and auction prices.

Beth Savino of Hobby Center Toys in Toledo, Ohio, sent Steiff Festival information and photos. I would also like to express my appreciation to the many unnamed festival guests and dealers who allowed me to photograph their Steiff toys. Some exhibitors are not included because I did not get their names.

Mike Underwood was very patient during our photography sessions, and the following dealers and others supplied photos or allowed me to photograph their Steiff: Dee Hockenberry, Cynthia Brintnall, Barbara Lauver, Harriet Purtill, Pamela Elkins, Lisa Vought, Bunny Walker, Rick and Jane Viprino, Dottie Ayers, Barbara Sykora, and Sue Potchen.

The Steiff Company could supply only limited material and information for this book because of an exclusive contract with Marianne and Jurgen Cieslik, whose book, *Knopf im Ohr,* was published earlier this year in German (an English translation is now available). Since these authors had free access to the Steiff archives, serious collectors will want to acquire this book (Theriault's, P.O. Box 151, Annapolis, MD 21201).

I have valued the friendship of Hans Otto Steiff and Jorg Junginger over the years, and I thank them for their past help. I also commend Dr. Herbert Zimmerman for continuing to uphold the tradition of Margarete Steiff by producing the high-quality toys we have come to know as Steiff.

Steiff TOYS REVISITED

Introduction

 Since the publication of *Steiff Teddy Bears, Dolls, and Toys* in 1984, many changes have taken place in the field of Steiff toys. It wasn't too long ago that good antiques shows would not allow Steiff toys to be included in dealers' exhibits, but now it is rare to find a show without them.

Well-known auction houses are featuring Steiff in toy sales and some even have had sales with teddy bears exclusively. Invariably the highest prices are paid for Steiff.

It is not unusual to see early Steiff teddies advertised for $2,000 to $3,000. Although the highest price known for one in 1983 was $5,000, many have been actually sold at considerably higher prices since then. A black Steiff teddy brought approximately $7,000 privately, and a record price paid for a teddy at auction was $7,100 at a sale conducted by Sotheby's in Chester, England, in 1986. Since that record, much higher prices have been paid.

In 1987 Richard Wright shocked the teddy bear world by paying more than $26,000 for two Steiff teddies with muzzles at another Sotheby's sale in London. At an auction I attended in Springfield, Ohio, in 1988, a 45″ Steiff teddy from 1905 brought the whopping price of $10,400, so who is to say what the future will bring?

The future is already here. After finishing the copy for this book I was in London, England, and heard about a Steiff teddy in Russian costume that was to be sold at Christie's on May 18. I went to Christie's South Kensington showrooms and saw the bear, which is shown in the color section. It was indeed a rare find.

The bear was the property of Xenia Georgievna, Princess of Russia, second cousin of Tzar Nicholas second. It was probably given to her by her father, George Mikhailovich, Grand Duke of Russia, who was assassinated in the Peter & Paul Fortress in 1919. Xenia was caught in England by the outbreak of the war in 1914 after a summer holiday at Buckingham Palace.

Another reason for the bear's rarity is the color. It is bright red mohair,

though worn in spots, and it has a Steiff button. Christie's dated it as 1906–1909 and stated in their catalogue that "the Steiff factory at Giengen have no records of making a line of red bears and suggest it was a special order made in very limited quantities." The teddy is 13" tall with an inoperative voice box and replaced front paws, which did not detract from the record price it brought of £12,100 or approximately $20,000. Steiff history is being rewritten constantly.

As this book was going to press, I heard the astonishing news that a Steiff teddy bear was sold at Sotheby's in London on September 19, 1989, for $86,000. It is from 1920 and is in superb condition. It has a mixture of blond and brown curly mohair, glass eyes measuring about one inch in diameter, and is 24" long (see page 72). Though the owner's name was not revealed, it was purchased by Jack Nisket for a private client in the U.S. The Russian bear is already scheduled to be sold as a limited edition replica by its purchaser, Ian Pout of Witney, England. It should be available in 1990.

More evidence of the interest in Steiff is the number of newsletters and price lists that are published regularly. I published a newsletter for two years called "Steiff Collectors' Anonymous," and dealers such as Barbara Lauver, Dee Hockenberry, and Harriet Purtill send out regular lists of old Steiff for sale. Hobby Center Toys of Toledo, Ohio, and Cynthia's Country Store of West Palm Beach, Florida, are just some dealers who publish regular newsletters with information about old toys and promotion of new ones. The area of Limited Editions and Collectors' Items produced by Steiff is also big business,

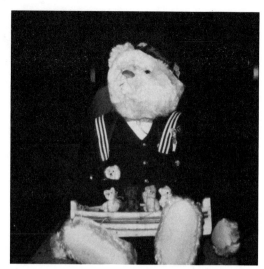

"Chester", a white Steiff teddy, broke the record for a teddy bear sold at auction at Sotheby's, London, in 1986, at more than $7,000.

Papa Bear is the most sought-after Collectors' Item produced by the Steiff Company. He was issued in 1980, with Mama and Baby appearing in 1981.

and this book will include a section that deals with them exclusively.

Many teddy bear conventions and other events where Steiff can be seen are held throughout the country. There is a big concentration of handcrafted bears at these events in addition to Steiff and other commercial brands.

The popularity of the magazine

Hans Otto Steiff, great-nephew of Margarete Steiff, spoke at the first two Festivals of Steiff.

Trunkful of original teddies and Margaret Strong Bears from the 1980s.

Small "Clownie" ponders imaginary travels with an antique globe just his size.

Puss-in-Boots from the 1950s has a well-loved look.

Two early red Steiff teddies came to the first Festival of Steiff with their owners, Paul McNabb and Susan Cashman.

Teddy, 3½″, with pewter button, in his own chair, c. 1905. Penguin, 3½″, from the 1950s, with miniature Teddy Roosevelt book.

Santa Claus with rubber head and hands, 1954, and "Rennie" Reindeer, 1957.

Teddy Bear and Friends is another indication of the continued interest in teddy bear memorabilia of all kinds. They too have a strong concentration of artist-made teddy bears and bear-related items in their publication.

Well-known authors such as Helen Sieverling, Linda Mullins, Margaret Fox Mandel, Dee Hockenberry, Patricia Schoonmaker, and the Bialovskys have all added to the information known about Steiff toys, but questions still arise concerning identification and dating of Steiff.

When my co-author of the first two books exclusively on Steiff toys, Shirley Conway, and I began our research for *100 Years of Steiff*, very little information was available. We used the historical material and photos sent by the Steiff Company, much of which had to be translated from German. We took pictures of our own collections and those of a few friends. That was in 1980.

Before publishing *Steiff Teddy Bears, Dolls, and Toys* four years later, we traveled to Giengen, Germany, and spent many hours in the Steiff Museum examining the bears and other animals and toys. The company supplied us with more information, some of which has not been accurate. Since that time, I have returned to Giengen twice for further research and have been in continual contact with the company and with the auction houses that have sold Steiff toys. I have also been accumulating old catalogues that were not shown in our other books and have bought and sold many Steiff toys.

The purpose of this book is to sort out the facts and to give collectors up-to-date information and examples of the Steiff toys that have appeared since the teddy bear renaissance began ten years ago. The inclusion of new catalogue

"Margit," a Limited Edition jointed doll with painted face, real hair, and leather shoes, 1987.

Original "Teddy Rose" from the Steiff Museum.

pages and a list of Collectors' Items and Limited Editions issued by Steiff, as well as a firsthand view of the first three Festivals of Steiff, should also be of interest to lovers of Steiff throughout the world.

Margarete Steiff and the History of the Steiff Company

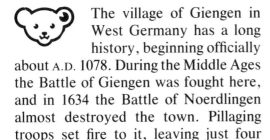 The village of Giengen in West Germany has a long history, beginning officially about A.D. 1078. During the Middle Ages the Battle of Giengen was fought here, and in 1634 the Battle of Noerdlingen almost destroyed the town. Pillaging troops set fire to it, leaving just four houses standing.

Farming and manual trades were the chief support of the villagers, and at the beginning of the nineteenth century the town contained 120 independent weavers, in addition to tanners, pewtersmiths, and other craftsmen. It was this heritage of skilled workmen that paved the way for the beginning of the toy factory that would make Giengen famous throughout the world, and it was one of its female citizens who was responsible for this fame.

In 1847 Margarete Steiff was born into this rural village surrounded by animals and farmland. Although she had polio as a child and was confined to a wheelchair, she had a sparkling personality and a strong determination to overcome her handicap. She learned dressmaking in the sewing school in Giengen,

and she and her sister had the first hand-driven sewing machine in Giengen. Because her right hand was lame, she turned the machine around so that she could turn the hand-wheel with her left hand.

Since her relatives owned a felt factory, Margarete decided to open a shop for making ready-made felt clothing. In addition to coats, dresses, and petticoats, the shop also made tablecloths and did tapestry work. The business was so successful that Margarete had to hire extra help. The shop was opened in 1877, and it was not long after that Margarete made the following entry in her notebook: "At this point the model of an elephant fell into my hands; felt was well suited to copying it. The finest shearings were used for the stuffing. This little

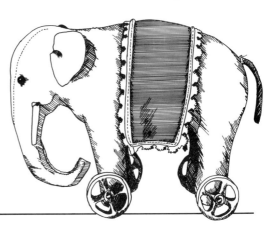

Margarete Steiff, the woman who made the small town of Giengen, Germany, famous.

A rayon plush teddy produced just after World War II.

One of many Steiff teddies produced in the early years.

felt elephant at first served as a pincushion.''

She gave the elephant away, possibly to her nephew Richard, and soon there were many demands for more from the neighborhood children. In 1880 she made eight elephants, and by 1886 the number of soft-stuffed toys made in her shop had risen to 5,066. She had added monkeys, donkeys, horses, pigs, and camels to the assortment. Margarete's brother Fritz sold them at country fairs.

A few years later sturdy frames were added to some animals, enabling them to be used as pull toys and for children to ride. As the demand for the animals grew, Margarete needed more space than her home would allow and she moved her business to a new location on Mill Street. Here she could sell the animals along with her other goods.

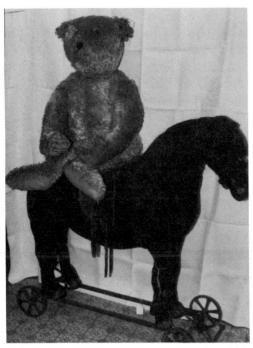

Steiff teddy, 48", and horse on wheels sold in 1988 by Bruce Knight at a Springfield, Ohio, auction (Courtesy Bruce Knight).

In 1893 an agent sold Steiff toys for the first time at the Leipzig Toy Fair, and the first Steiff catalogue was published. A traveling salesman was hired, and Margarete ventured into new designs, such as dolls made with felt bodies and felt clothing.

Richard Steiff, Margarete's nephew, joined the firm in 1897 after studying art in Stuttgart and England. In 1903 he suggested construction of the first all-window building for the business. It had a working area of 10,000 square feet and was the model for future buildings added by the company. Richard's major contribution, however, was a bear with movable arms and legs, a prototype for

Felt dolls with pressed-felt heads from the 1930s (Courtesy Wolf's Toy Store, Giengen).

Steiff circus bear, 1920 (Courtesy Wolf's Toy Store, Giengen).

a toy that eventually came to be known as the "teddy bear." Richard designed the teddy bear from drawings he had made as he watched bears in the Stuttgart zoo.

For the first time mohair plush was used for toy animals, making them more realistic. Mohair plush is made from the fur of the angora goat, an animal native to the Cape of Good Hope and Turkey. It is specially treated and spun into yarn, which is woven into cotton-backed mohair plush on special looms.

The bear's popularity zoomed after an American buyer ordered 3,000 at the Leipzig Toy Fair. It is rumored, though the White House cannot substantiate the story, that the bears were used as table decorations for a wedding party at the White House because of Teddy Roosevelt's love for hunting bears. This is how the bears became known as "teddies."

In 1903, the Steiff Company made 12,000 bears. Soon two other nephews, Paul and Franz Steiff, as well as three nieces, had joined the firm. Franz Steiff represented the company at the Columbian Exposition in Saint Louis in 1904, and two years later, in 1906, the company was registered in Stuttgart, with Margarete Steiff and her three nephews as founders. That same year Hugo Steiff joined the company as an engineer. He planned and installed mass-production methods and supervised manufacturing and the construction of the new factory.

In 1907, the company made 974,000 bears, but the year was a bad one because business reverses in America forced the cancellation of many orders. Fortunately, through the ingenuity of its management, the company survived and in 1908 more than a million Steiff bears were exported.

Richard Steiff's development of the Roloplan, a tailless kite, as well as new dolls with stuffed felt bodies and bears with automatic growlers and tumbling mechanisms, helped to overcome the crisis the company experienced in 1907, but in 1909 Margarete succumbed to the ill health that had plagued her all her life.

Margarete's nephews continued to operate the company according to her high standards. Otto Steiff had joined the company in 1902, taking over the business management and advertising. He founded the firms of Steiff Frères in Paris in 1911 and Margarete Steiff & Company in New York in 1912.

An artist named Schlopsnies was hired by the company to design the display pieces that were so important in the promotion of Steiff toys through the years and that are now mechanized. Schlopsnies also designed an unusual doll for Steiff that bears his name. It has a jointed felt body with a celluloid head made by another company. These dolls are rare, and the only one I have seen was at the Steiff Museum.

World War I reduced production at the Steiff plant. Because the company could not obtain materials for its regular line of animals, it started to make blocks and children's wood furniture. After the war the company put a scooter into mass production, and the increased popularity of dogs and cats led to such creations as "Molly," "Charly," "Bully," and "Fluffy."

Richard Steiff moved to America to deal with the problems of inflation and export difficulties. Animals on eccentric wheels such as "Record Peter" and children's vehicles, along with the scooter, broadened the company's market. Margarete Steiff GmbH prospered and improved methods of production until a world economic crisis occurred in the late 1920s. Management struggled to keep its skilled workers and to maintain the quality that had become the trademark of the company.

In 1930 the company founded by Margarete Steiff celebrated its fiftieth anniversary, but by the end of the decade the reign of Adolph Hitler had made its mark on the veteran firm. Friendly countries were supplied with toys on a small scale until mohair became impossible to obtain. The factory closed in 1943. After the war few workers were left who knew the art of making the stuffed toys and it was difficult to resume production. Rayon plush was substituted for the unavailable mohair, but customers continued to demand the pre-war materials of Steiff.

In 1948 mohair plush again became available and the Steiff company returned to the manufacture of its former models. The first exhibition in fifteen years was held in New York in 1949, and gradually the company was able to recapture its place in the competitive world of stuffed toys.

The development of a line of miniatures spurred sales, and the introduction of a figure called "Mecki" in 1950 was also significant. "Mecki" was a hedgehog with a body of felt and a head of cast rubber, a technique that was expanded to many other figures, such as a family of "Meckis," dwarfs, and the Santa Claus.

Margarete Steiff's innovative trademark for her toys, represented by a metal button in the left ear, was to

Rare "Petsey" with curly mohair fur and blue glass eyes, c. 1928 (Courtesy Pamela Elkins).

Early clown dolls from the Steiff Museum.

prove ingenious. The trademark "Button in Ear" (in German, *Knopf im Ohr*) became synonymous with Steiff all over the world and was her assurance that "For our children the best is only good enough." Customers associate this button with the quality that has been typical of Steiff toys since the company began.

The first Steiff catalogue was printed in 1893. Succeeding catalogues contained some color illustrations, but the first full-color catalogue did not appear until the 1950s. The years after World War II were the best ever for the Steiff Company, and the introduction of Collectors' Items and Limited Editions in 1980 has been the impetus for even more sales.

The company is now under the direction of Dr. Herbert Zimmerman. Jorg Junginger, a descendant of the Steiff family, is currrently the manager of development and design.

Margarete Steiff now lies in her grave in Giengen, but if she were alive to see the joy she has brought to children and adults all over the world, I am sure she would smile and say, "I told you so."

Identifying and Dating Steiff Toys

 Much has been written about the identification and dating of Steiff toys by the trademark "Button in Ear" and other tags, and the Steiff Company itself has made some discoveries in its research that were not known at the time Shirley Conway and I were writing *Steiff Teddy Bears, Dolls, and Toys* (1984). I will try to give the most up-to-date information that the company has shared with me.

We know that Margarete Steiff wanted to establish a trademark that would be unique and make her toys stand out from others, and also to assure her customers that they could be guaranteed good quality. That is why she started attaching buttons to the left ears of her toys.

In 1904 the Steiff company issued a pamphlet with the statement: "Trade mark (elephant with a trunk shaped like an *S*) which, as of November 1, 1904, I will attach to each item without exception, i.e. in the left ear on a small button of nickel. Legal protection has been applied for regarding this kind of attachment." This button was 6 mm in diameter with the elephant appearing to the left. A blank button may also have been attached to some toys during this same period.

The elephant was eventually replaced on the button and thereafter the Steiff name was printed in block letters.

The earlier buttons have the final "F" in "Steiff" extending back under the name. Buttons with this trademark in diameters of 4, 5, 6, and 8 mm were also made. The letters are raised on the metal and can be felt by rubbing.

During World War II, because of a shortage of material, the button was no longer galvanized or nickeled but still had a gray metal color. This may be when the Steiff name was no longer underlined.

In 1950 the block letters were replaced by script, which was also raised, on a shiny chrome button in diameters of 4, 6, 8, and 15 mm. The buttons were

Elephant trademark on button, 1904.

First bear tademark with button showing printed and underlined name.

Steiff script logo with round bear, introduced in 1950.

attached with a claw rivet. About 1965 the company changed the shape of the button to a convex top with the script letters incised into the metal.

An 8 mm brass button in two pieces with a plain surface with recessed letters was introduced in 1977. In 1982 a 9 mm button of the same type was introduced. For toys of secondary quality, such as those sold in the Steiff Company store at reduced prices, the brass button is still attached, but it is plain and has no trademark.

The different trademark styles are confusing because exceptions exist. I have had animals with small brass buttons with raised script letters that I am sure were from the late 1970's, and the company makes no mention of that button. It also does not mention the blank button, but we have all seen too many of those to know that they were used.

A protective tag has also been attached to the ear of Steiff toys along with the button. Originally the color of the tag was white with black lettering. In 1926 the color was changed to red or orange, and in 1934 it became yellow. Since 1979 the tag has been made of a woven material with red lettering.

Most Steiff toys also had a cardboard tag attached to the front of the animals. The original tags were white, showing the name and the number of the toy and the words "Steiff Original." Around 1925 the tag was changed to include a bear's head. This tag has a red margin with a pink background. The bear's head is squared and his rounded mouth extends beyond the bottom of the circle.

In 1950 the bear's head on the tag became rounded, and the chin still extends beyond the bottom. Since 1972 the tag has been completely round with

Logo used by Steiff today.

red and yellow lettering. The Limited Editions, which have been made since 1980, have white tags.

Unfortunately, many of these cardboard tags have been removed over the years, but sometimes the thread is still visible where one was attached, giving a clue to its authenticity as Steiff. The same is true of the buttons. Although they were more difficult to remove, many were taken out by overprotective parents or zealous children. It is sometimes possible to see the holes where the button was attached, especially if the ear is made of felt.

Other clues to dating Steiff toys have to do with customs laws. When "Made in Germany" or "Importe de Allemagne" appears on a tag, it means it was exported after 1914, when the customs laws changed to make the name of the country of export and "Made in" essential. A tag that just says "Germany" indicates dates between 1891 and 1914. Some toys have tags that say "Made in U.S. Zone Germany." This indicates the years just after World War II. Of course if the toy was purchased

in Germany, customs laws would not apply.

Each toy has a style number that should be printed on the ear tag. Until 1970 the number and size of the toy were separated by a comma; since that time a slash has replaced the comma. An explanation of the style numbers is also helpful. Before the numbering system was changed to a slash one could figure the position, covering, size, and accessories of the toy by the number.

The first digit refers to the posture of the animal (standing or lying). The second digit indicates the covering used, such as felt or mohair. The third and fourth digits give the size of the toy in centimeters. The digits after the comma or slash mark indicate the accessories or extra additions, such as wheels, voice, or music box.

For example, a camel from the 1950s has the following number: 1514,0. It is standing (1), has a wool plush covering (5), is 14 centimeters high, and has no accessories.

At some point in the 1960s, the method of numbering appears to have changed. The size of the toy, in centimeters, now comes after the slash mark.

The best source for identifying and dating old Steiff is old company catalogues. Unfortunately they are hard to

Cardboard tags used since the 1920s: c. 1925, 1950, and 1972 (Reprinted from *Steiff Teddy Bears, Dolls, and Toys.* Drawings by Tecla Powell).

find. A special section of this book reproduces pages from the 1955, 1957, 1959, and 1960 catalogues. Others can be found in the book *Steiff Teddy Bears, Dolls, and Toys*.

An interesting bit of information surfaced at the 1988 Steiff festival when Jorg Junginger told us that center-seam Steiff teddies are not necessarily older than teddies without the seam. He said that they were made as late as the 1920s whenever material was in short supply. This is just one example of how facts concerning the production and dating of Steiff can be so confusing. Most collectors believe that the center-seam Steiff teddies are the oldest and most desirable.

The "Festivals of Steiff"

 The first Festival of Steiff was held in Toledo, Ohio, in 1986. It was organized by Hobby Center Stores and their owners, Beth and Ben Savino. Headquarters for the first and subsequent festivals and for the 1989 festival was the Hotel Sofitel on the lakefront in downtown Toledo.

Except for one day, the festival is not aimed at the general public. Registered guests are treated to elegant dinners, wine and cheese parties, and, at the 1987 and 1988 festivals, an auction of Steiff items.

The most sophisticated dealers and collectors attend the festival, along with important figures in the field of Steiff. Hans Otto Steiff attended the first two sessions, accompanied one year by his son. Because of Steiff's ill health in 1988, Jorg Junginger represented the company. He is responsible for the Steiff Museum in Giengen, Germany, and is also in charge of the archives, which hold many of the mysteries involving old Steiff toys. He personally took the pictures in the museum which we used in *Steiff Teddy Bears, Dolls, and Toys*. Other notable personalities who have attended the festivals are Gary Ruddell, publisher of *Teddy Bear and Friends* magazine; Gerald Fischer, president of Reeves, International, the distributor of Steiff in this country; Richard Frantz, area representative for Reeves; and Rosemary and Paul Volpp, internationally known collectors.

Selected dealers display their wares to an exclusive clientele, and the most expensive Steiff toys in the world have been seen on display. Barbara Lauver, Lisa Vought, Dee Hockenberry and Lorraine Oakley, Richard Wright, Rick and Jane Viprino, D & D Productions, Gay Gressman, and Mike Connolly are just a few of these dealers.

In 1986 Lorraine Freisberg brought the Steiff bear she had just purchased in Chester, England, for $7,100. That was the record price for a teddy bear sold at auction at that time. The bear, who was named "Chester," was kept in a cabinet for years and was never played with, which accounted for its excellent condition. She had dressed the teddy in a child's sailor suit, which added to its appeal.

In 1987 Richard Wright brought the pair of muzzled white teddies that he purchased at Sotheby's London auction house for more than $26,000. He also

brought a white teddy, for which he paid $1,400 at the same sale.

The festival offers a variety of informative programs and a contest in which prizes are awarded for such categories as "Best Dressed Bear," "Most Appealing Vintage Bear," "Most Appealing Vintage Animal," and "Most Unusual Steiff." Having acted as a judge for the past three years, I can attest to the difficulty of the job because of the great variety of unusual pieces entered in the contest.

Beth Savino, an accomplished collector herself, always displays her fantastic assortment of old Steiff, as well as the new Steiff line sold by Hobby Center Stores. In addition, the Steiff Company sends animals from its archives to be displayed at the festival, some of them on display for the first time. One year Mr. Steiff showed movies of the celebration in Giengen, Germany, in 1953 on the occasion of the 50th anniversary of the teddy bear.

On Sunday afternoon the displays are open to the public for a fee, and Mr. Steiff graciously talked to people and autographed their Steiff toys when he was able to attend.

At the auction of old toys during the 1988 festival, some interesting items appeared. Two pandas from the late 1940s or early 1950s, reminiscent of those on display at the Toledo Zoo at the same time, sold for $510, an 11″ Teddy Baby from the 1950s brought $550, and a Papa Bear from 1980 was sold for $650.

A fourth Festival of Steiff was held in Toledo in June of 1989 with the usual attendance of Steiff celebrities, dealers, and collectors. Jorg Junginger attended for the second year and brought with him some remarkable specimens from the Steiff Museum Collection. A Father Christmas doll from 1913 and a Santa Claus in a sleigh with eight reindeer from the 1950s were especially interesting.

The contest brought forth some most unusual Steiff pieces. First prize in this category was awarded for an airplane called "Stratosplan" which had swastikas on the tail. Another fascinating item was a board which had been prepared by the company for salesmen to use as a sales pitch to emphasize the quality of Steiff teddy bears. It shows the separate parts which are put together to make a teddy including arms, legs, ears, etc. Junginger explained to me that he had designed the board during the 1970s.

The Saturday night auction was as exciting as ever, and on Sunday the public could attend to see the old and new Steiff items which were on display and for sale. The Savinos are never sure from year to year whether the festival will be repeated, but the continued interest in Steiff will surely call for repetition of this event in some way.

Jorg Junginger signs a teddy bear at the festival.

Rare bowling or "kugel" set on sale at the 1988 festival.

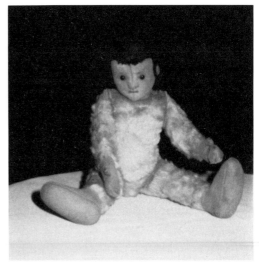

"Most Unusual Toy" winner at the first Steiff festival.

A prize-winner in the "Most Unusual Toy" contest at the 1988 festival.

Lifesize doll on display at the festival.

Hobby Center Toy's Beth Savino with a Steiff rabbit.

A prize-winner in "Most Appealing" category at the 1988 festival.

"Musicanto" Santa Claus with music box on sale at the festival for $1,800.

First prize-winner in the "Most Appealing Teddy" at the 1988 festival.

Early soldier doll on sale at the 1988 festival.

Appealing Steiff teddy exhibited by D & D Productions at the 1988 festival.

White teddy, 14", exhibited by D & D Productions at the 1988 festival.

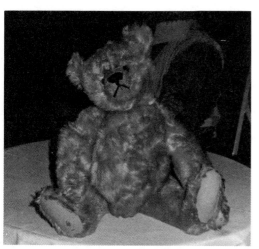

Wonderful Steiff teddy purchased at Marvin Cohen Auctions by Bunny Walker.

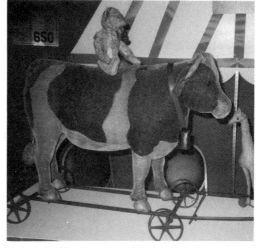

Large Steiff cow on wheels exhibited at the 1988 festival (exhibitor unknown).

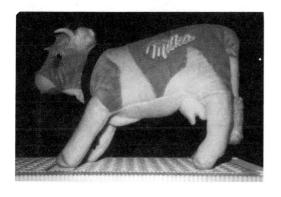

Steiff cow made as an advertising item for a chocolate company (exhibitor unknown).

Rare Humpty Dumpty felt toy shown in Steiff's 1913 catalogue (Courtesy Lisa Vought).

Original Mickey Mouse, 1932, from the Steiff Museum.

Mechanical cat and mouse from the 1950s brought to the 1988 festival by Bunnie Walker for auction.

Mint condition 17" Teddy Baby on sale at the 1988 festival for $1,350 (exhibitor unknown).

"Bo" and "Dearheart," famous teddies owned by Rosemary and Paul Volpp, were all dressed up for the 1988 festival.

Steiff festival prize-winner in "Most Appealing" category (owner unknown).

Darling early gold teddy on display at the 1988 festival (exhibitor unknown).

Display at festival: Teddy with removable hot water bottle.

Steiff at Auction

The prestigious firm of Sotheby's had its first sale of teddy bears in 1983, but the sale did not include any Steiff teddies. The success of that sale, along with publicity received from the television production of *Brideshead Revisited,* the craze for teddy bears in the United States, and Peter Bull's *The Teddy Bear Book* and *A Hug of Teddy Bears,* led the London branch of Sotheby's to arrange succeeding sales.

Since that sale, Sotheby's has seen many world records for the sale of teddy bears. Bunny Campione, Sotheby's expert on dolls and teddies, predicts that the next record will be set by an early black Steiff teddy, if one can be found.

The record before 1989 was for a large muzzled bear purchased by Richard Wright in 1987 for $14,960. He also bought another one in a smaller size, bringing the total price for the pair to more than $26,000.

That record has been broken twice in 1989. The first was $20,000 for a red Steiff teddy at Christie's South Kensington in London. It was purchased by Ian Pout, an English teddy bear dealer who plans to exhibit it in his museum at Witney. He will also sell a replica which is being made by the Steiff Company. That record was soundly broken when Jack Nisbet paid $86,000 at Sotheby's in London for a 1920 dual-plush teddy, purchased for an unidentified American buyer.

Other auction houses have followed Sotheby's and Christie's. Marvin Cohen of New Lebanon, Pennsylvania, has also conducted several sales with very good Steiff items, and Bruce Knight of Springfield, Ohio, has sold some wonderful Steiff at his Christmas auctions. It was at his 1988 auction that a 45″ Steiff teddy bear from 1905 brought the price of $10,400.

Many of the Steiff toys that are purchased at auctions surface later at antique and toy shows. The Brimfield, Massachusetts, shows are noted for their abundance of good Steiff on sale, and most good shows have at least one old Steiff on display.

The following pages show a selection of these items that have actually been sold at auction, with descriptions, year of sale, and prices (when available). Prices include the 10 percent pre-

Gold plush teddy, 24", center seam, growler, button, c. 1904, **$3,896** (1986). Courtesy Sotheby's.

mium paid at most auction houses. From sales in England, prices are figured at the rate of the British pound at the time of the sale, rounded off to the nearest dollar. In some cases the value of the pound at the time of the sale was unavailable.

Gold plush teddy, 12½", c. 1908, some wear, **$762** (1986). Courtesy Sotheby's.

Orange plush teddy, 11", button, c. 1906, wear and moth damage, est. **$500–$800** (no sale price given, 1986). Courtesy Sotheby's.

Blonde plush teddy with glass eyes, 23", button, c. 1920, stitching frayed, **$2,541** (1986). Courtesy Sotheby's.

Orange plush teddy, 16½", button, c. 1910, moth damage and repairs, **$847** (1986). Courtesy Sotheby's.

Beige plush teddy, 27", button, c. 1907, wear, **$2,202** (1986). Courtesy Sotheby's.

Mohair jack rabbit with velvet clothes, 12½", script button, c. 1960, with small teddy, **$430** (1986). Courtesy Sotheby's.

Blonde plush teddy, 24", growler, button, c. 1908, wear, **$1,779** (1986). Courtesy Sotheby's.

Gold plush teddy, 21¼", c. 1904, moth damage, **$1,948** (1986). Courtesy Sotheby's.

White plush teddy, 16½″, button, c. 1904, excellent condition, **$3,388** (1986). Courtesy Sotheby's.

Cinnamon long plush teddy, 24″, growler, button, c. 1905, wear and repairs, **$1,525** (1986). Courtesy Sotheby's.

Orange plush teddy, 27", button, c. 1904, wear and moth damage, **$3,388**. Courtesy Sotheby's.

White plush polar bear, 17¾" long, with swivel head, growler, button, c. 1925, wear, **$1,525,** Courtesy Sotheby's.

Blonde mechanical bear, left arm winds for somersaults, 13", button, c. 1908, wear, **$880** (1986). Courtesy Sotheby's.

Blonde plush teddy, 29", growler, c. 1904, much wear, **$1,779** (1986). Courtesy Sotheby's.

Yellow plush teddy, 13½", button, c. 1908, wear and repairs, **$915** (1986). Courtesy Sotheby's.

Gold plush teddy, 24", growler, c. 1910, wear, **$2,464** (1986). Courtesy Sotheby's.

Sailor doll with felt body and leather boots with Steiff buttons, 20", c. 1924, **$1,085** (1986).
Courtesy Sotheby's.

Beige plush teddy, 27½″, button, c. 1908, **$3,344** (1986). Courtesy Sotheby's.

Left: Blonde long plush teddy, 24", growler, c. 1907, wear, **$1,936** (1986). *Right:* Yellow plush teddy, 20", button, c. 1920, wear, **$792** (1986). Courtesy Sotheby's.

Yellow plush teddy, 13$\frac{1}{2}$", growler, c. 1915, moth damage and wear, **$396** (1986). Courtesy Sotheby's.

Left: Rust plush teddy, 11", growler, button, c. 1925, wear, **$396** (1986). *Right:* Yellow plush teddy, 8", button, c. 1920, wear, **$444.** Courtesy Sotheby's.

Gold plush teddy, 18", button, c. 1907, moth damage, **$1,109** (1986). Courtesy Sotheby's.

Left: Brown plush teddy, 11", button, c. 1909, moth damage, **$636** (1986). *Center (front):* Tan plush teddy, 10", button, c. 1905, foot pads replaced, **$308**. *Left (back):* Tan plush teddy, 15¾", button, c. 1905, wear and moth damage, **$430**. *Right (front):* Beige plush teddy, 10", button, c. 1910, with small Shuco bear, **$412** (1986). (Bear in sweater not Steiff.) Courtesy Sotheby's.

Brown plush riding bear, 16½", pull-string, growler, button, c. 1935, **$285** (1986). Courtesy Sotheby's.

Blonde plush teddy, 29", button, c. 1905, wear, **$1,742** (1986). Courtesy Sotheby's.

Two felt dolls, each with button, c. 1913, wear: Fat man in blue felt uniform with knapsack and heavy black leather walking boots, 11". Girl, with blue eyes and blonde hair, in white top, black jodphurs, and tan walking boots, 14", **$2,112** (1987). Courtesy Sotheby's.

Beige plush teddy, 27″, growler, c. 1905, moth damage, **$3,784** (1986). Courtesy Sotheby's.

Blonde plush teddy, 13¾", button, c. 1907, holes in pads, **$634** (1986). Courtesy Sotheby's.

Pair of beige long plush teddies, 13½", button, c. 1907, wear, **$4,400** (1987). Courtesy Sotheby's.

Orange plush teddy, 25", c. 1908, repairs, **$2,464** (1987). Courtesy Sotheby's.

Blonde plush teddy, 12½", growler, button, c. 1904, wear, est. £700–900 (no sale price given, 1987). Courtesy Sotheby's.

Gold plush teddy, 20", growler, c. 1905, wear, **$1,742** (1986). Felt doll with felt clothes, 38", c. 1913, moth damage, **$1,109** (1986). Courtesy Sotheby's.

Blonde plush teddy, 24½", growler, button, c. 1908, wear, no sale price given (1987). Courtesy Sotheby's.

Yellow plush teddy, 11½", button, c. 1934, moth damage, **$1,739** (1987). Courtesy Sotheby's.

Yellow plush teddy, 14", button, c. 1913, moth damage, **$876** (1987). Courtesy Sotheby's.

White plush teddy, 20½", center seam, c. 1904, wear, **$1,460** (1987). Courtesy Sotheby's.

Blond plush teddy, 16 ½", growler, c. 1913, **$1,850** (1987). Courtesy Sotheby's.

Yellow plush teddy, 27", c. 1907, wear, **$1,752** (1987). Courtesy Sotheby's.

Pair of felt dolls with glass eyes and felt clothing, 10½", c. 1913, **$832**. Courtesy Sotheby's.

Yellow plush teddy, 19", center seam, growler, button, c. 1904, wear, **$3,310** (1987). Courtesy Sotheby's.

Pair of felt dolls with glass eyes and felt clothing, 10½", c. 1913, **$1,848** (1987). Courtesy Sotheby's.

Felt doll with felt clothing and Steiff buttons on vest, 13", c. 1915, **$3,142** (1987).
Courtesy Sotheby's.

Blonde plush teddy, 29", button, c. 1903, wear and repairs, **$4,283** (1987). Courtesy Sotheby's.

Blonde plush teddy, 25", button, c. 1904, wear and repairs, **$3,894**. Courtesy Sotheby's.

Orange plush teddy, 12½", growler, button, c. 1908, repairs, **$799** (1987). Courtesy Sotheby's.

Orange plush teddy, 27", growler, c. 1908, wear, **$1,427** (1987). Courtesy Sotheby's.

Orange plush teddy, 16", c. 1904, wear and repairs, **$1,237**. Courtesy Sotheby's.

Dual-tone plush teddy, 11½", center seam, glass eyes, growler, button, c. 1928, **$952**. Courtesy Sotheby's.

Blonde plush teddy, 27½", button, c. 1904, wear, **$7,788** (1987). Courtesy Sotheby's.

Cinnamon plush teddy, 15", button, c. 1908, wear and repairs, **$723**. Courtesy Sotheby's.

Yellow plush teddy, 24", growler, button, c. 1905, wear, est. £1,500–2,000 (no sale price given, 1987). Courtesy Sotheby's.

Blonde plush teddy, metal rod construction, 16",
elephant button, c. 1903, nose partly missing,
wear, est. £1,200–1,800 (no sale price given,
1987). Courtesy Sotheby's.

Blonde plush teddy, 24", button, c. 1908, wear,
$4,948 (1987). Courtesy Sotheby's.

Blonde plush teddy, 20", growler, button, c. 1908,
wear and repairs, est. £800–1,200 (no sale price
given, 1987). Courtesy Sotheby's.

Blonde plush teddy muff, 13½", kidskin pads, c.
1908, wear, **$609** (1987). Courtesy Sotheby's.

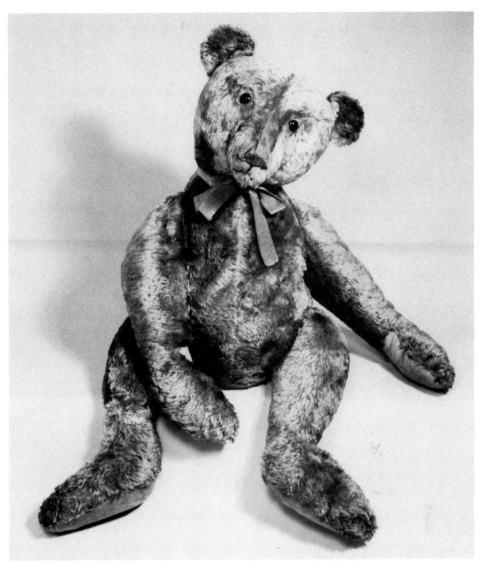

Blonde plush teddy, 45", growler, button, c. 1904, wear, **$5,709** (1987).
Courtesy Sotheby's.

Blonde plush teddy, 27", growler, button, c. 1905, wear, **$4,567** (1987). Courtesy Sotheby's.

White plush pig with glass eyes, $8\frac{1}{2}''$ by 15", button, c. 1913, contains holes, **$666.** Velvet cat with glass eyes and bell, $4'' \times 9\frac{1}{2}''$, elephant button, c. 1903–4, wear, **$933** (1987). Courtesy Sotheby's.

Left: Blonde plush teddy, $24\frac{1}{2}''$, button, c. 1908, wear and repairs, **$1,237,** with small bear (not Steiff). Courtesy Sotheby's.

White plush teddy, 16", blank button, c. 1903–4, wear and repairs, **$2,093** (1987). Courtesy Sotheby's.

Felt swan on steel frame and wheels, 10½" long, c. 1908, **$3,683** (1988). Courtesy Sotheby's.

Gold plush teddy, metal rod construction, elephant button, c. 1904, part of nose missing, wear, **$3,274** (1988). Courtesy Sotheby's.

Collage of Steiff Collectors' Items (Courtesy Cynthia Brintnall).

Two muzzle bears held the record for Steiff teddies sold at auction until this year (Courtesy Sotheby's, London).

Cinnamon mohair teddy, 24", with printed button, c. 1906 (Courtesy Sue Potchen).

White curly mohair teddy, 24", c. 1950 (Courtesy Barbara Lauver).

"Archibald," a 27" Steiff teddy sold at Sotheby's in 1987 for $8,152 (Courtesy Sotheby's, London).

A 1982 Richard Steiff bear with a 1987 Steiff doll at a tea party complete with silver service.

The three bears (3½″, 5″, and 6½″) cook their porridge, c. 1950s.

Felt doll, 13", sold at Christie's in 1988 for £ 880, along with early Steiff teddy bear (Courtesy Christie's, London).

"The West End Gang": Five Steiff teddies, each about 10" high. Only one has an underlined button. All have been loved and discarded but have been repaired, dressed, and loved again (Courtesy Bunny Walker).

Early clown doll with elephant button, 1905, and sailor doll. The sailor has jointed knees and Steiff buttons on the shoes. Exhibited by Barbara Lauver at the Steiff festival.

Six miniature teddies ready for a trip in their own trunk.

A distinguished assortment of old Steiff bears for sale at the Steiff festival (Courtesy Hobby Center Toys).

Beautiful assortment of Steiff teddies in costume, exhibited at the Steiff festival by The Calico Teddy.

Rare Steiff teddy, sold at Christie's South Kensington in London for the record price of £ 12,100, about $20,000. It was owned by a Russian princess who was in England at the outbreak of the Russian Revolution, thus possibly escaping assassination along with her cousins Tzar Nicholas and his family. It is dressed in Russian clothes, but the other unusual feature is its bright red mohair covering. The Steiff Company told Christie's that it has no record of making a line of red bears and suggests it was a special order made in very limited quantities (Courtesy Christie's South Kensington).

Left: White plush teddy with glass eyes, 13", button, c. 1930, **$1,637**. *Right:* White plush teddy, 18", growler, button, c. 1935, wear, **$1,432**. Courtesy Sotheby's.

Steiff doll trio with felt clothing and buttons, wool hair, and instruments, two Steiff buttons, c. 1911, est. **£6,000–8,000** (no sale price given, 1988). Courtesy Sotheby's.

Blonde plush teddy, 28¼", growler, button, c. 1908, some wear, **$1,739** (1988). Courtesy Sotheby's.

Gold plush teddy with glass eyes, 18", growler, button, c. 1935, one eye missing, **$818** (1988). Courtesy Sotheby's.

Gold plush teddy, 16", button, c. 1904, wear, **$1,944.** Courtesy Sotheby's.

Left: Gold plush teddy, 15", button and blank button, c. 1904, **$6,547.** *Middle:* Long white plush teddy with glass eyes, 24", button, c. 1920, wear, **$2,251.** *Right:* Beige plush teddy, 29", growler, button, c. 1905, wear, **$9,207** (1988). Courtesy Sotheby's.

Gold plush teddy, 30", growler, c. 1907, much wear, **$979** (1988). Courtesy Sotheby's.

Cinnamon curly plush Teddy Baby, 62", c. 1948, slight wear, **$1,664** (1988). Courtesy Sotheby's.

Blonde plush teddy, 20", growler, button, c. 1908, wear and repairs, **$3,887** (1988).
Courtesy Sotheby's.

Blonde plush teddy, 18½", with three photos of owners, center seam, c. 1906, wear, **$3,069** (1988). Courtesy Sotheby's.

White plush teddy with glass eyes, 21", growler, button, c. 1920, wear, **$2,154** (1988). Courtesy Sotheby's.

Gold plush teddy, 28", growler, c. 1904, wear, **$5,091** (1988). Courtesy Sotheby's.

White curly plush teddy with glass eyes, 25",
growler, button, c. 1925, **$2,864** (1988). Cour-
tesy Sotheby's.

Gold plush teddy, 29", growler, button, c. 1904,
wear and repairs, **$3,720** (1988). Courtesy
Sotheby's.

Cinnamon plush teddy, 16", button removed,
c. 1903, wear, **$1,664** (1988). Courtesy Sothe-
by's.

Blonde plush teddy, 20", growler, button, c. 1904,
wear. Price unavailable (with Käthe Kruse doll),
1988. Courtesy Sotheby's.

Blonde plush teddy with leather muzzle, 20½", growler, button removed, c. 1913, **$2,545** (1988). Courtesy Sotheby's.

Gold plush teddy, 19", growler, button, c. 1920, **$3,133** (1988). Courtesy Sotheby's.

White plush teddy with leather muzzle, 17¾, growler, button, c. 1913, **$3,329** (1988).
Courtesy Sotheby's.

Cinnamon plush teddy, 20", button removed, c. 1904, some wear, **$4,699** (1988). Courtesy Sotheby's.

Cinnamon plush teddy, 25″, growler, button, c. 1935, wear, **$3,133** (1988). Courtesy Sotheby's.

Felt doll ("Strewel Peter") with blue glass eyes, wig, and felt clothing, 19½″, c. 1913, **£1,220** (1986). Courtesy Christie's.

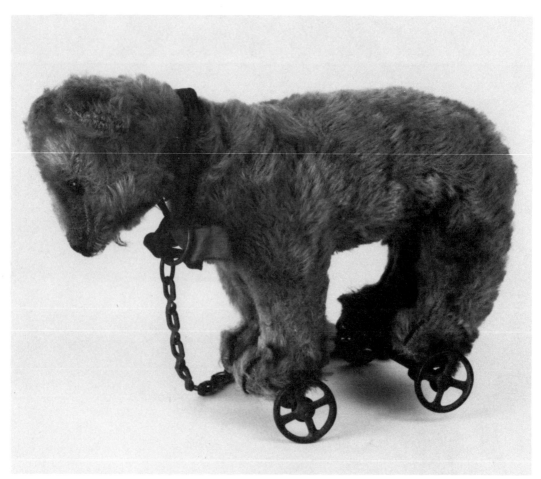

Honey plush bear on metal wheels with collar and chain, 6″ tall, c. 1908, £315 (1987). Courtesy Christie's.

Left: White plush polar bear, 15″ long, growler, c. 1925, price unavailable. *Right:* Blonde plush teddy, 13″, growler, button missing, **£330** (1988). Courtesy Christie's.

These teddies all look like Steiff except the one standing in back. The only one with a button is on the right: pale gold, 24″, growler, c. 1909, **$1,650** (1986). Courtesy Christie's.

Blonde plush teddy, 32", growler, button, **£682** (1988). Courtesy Christie's.

Honey plush teddy, center seam, growler, no button, c. 1908, **£770** (1988). Courtesy Christie's.

Silver plush teddy, 14", button, **£550** (1988). Courtesy Christie's.

Gold plush fox with glass eyes and swivel head and legs, 20" long, button, **£220** (1988). Courtesy Christie's.

Velvet rabbit with original blue felt jacket and leather-soled slippers, rattle inside, 13", c. 1905, **£165** (1988). Courtesy Christie's.

Honey plush teddy, 13½″, button, moth damage, **£440** (1988). Courtesy Christie's.

Gold plush teddy, 29", button, wear, **£2,860** (1988). Courtesy Christie's.

White plush polar bear with jointed hips and swivel head, c. 1913, **£385** (1988). Courtesy Christie's.

Strawberry blonde plush teddy, blank button, c. 1903, wear, **£528** (1988). Courtesy Christie's.

Early blonde plush teddy, 17", growler, button, wear, **£440**. Courtesy Christie's.

Early gray wool elephant with red felt blanket, 8″ tall, on metal wheels, **£240** (1988). Courtesy Christie's.

Gold plush teddy, 19½″, c. 1920, **£830** (1988). Courtesy Christie's.

Bunny Campione, Sotheby's doll and teddy bear expert, holding a dual-plush Steiff bear, German, c. 1920. This teddy sold on September 19, 1989, at Sotheby's for a record price of £55,000 (Courtesy Sotheby's).

Jack Nisbet, chairman of the House of Nisbet, fondles the $86,000 Steiff teddy he purchased on behalf of a private client in the U.S.

Collectors' Items: Limited Editions and Replicas

 Since 1980, the Steiff company has introduced replicas from their archives. These replicas, which have fast become collectors' items, are made in a limited edition and then discontinued. The idea, which has been highly successful, is to reproduce popular toys from past production, since old Steiff toys have become so popular and hard to find in this country.

It all began in 1980 with the Papa Bear, which was produced to celebrate the centennial of the Steiff Company. Steiff produced 5,000 of these bears to sell in the United States. Each was numbered and presented in a special box. The limited edition of Papa Bear sold for $150 in 1980. Now these bears bring as much as $900 or more.

Because of Papa Bear's popularity with collectors, the following year Steiff produced a Mama Bear and Baby Bear, creating a whole bear family. Since then, the Steiff Company has produced an array of limited mohair editions along with some other, unlimited Collector's Items. These new items have created a whole new field for Steiff collectors and are the leading best-sellers for the company.

Cynthia Brintnall, president of Cynthia's Country Store, Inc., of West Palm Beach, Florida has compiled a list of the limited editions with their current prices. I wish to thank Cynthia for her efforts and for sharing the list with us. She also supplied the full-page collage picture of Collectors' Items in the color section.

ITEM NUMBER	YEAR	NAME	PRICE

01543,43   1980   Papa Jubilee Bear $900 up

Limited to 11,000 worldwide, 5,000 USA. White tag, numbered, and boxed with certificate.

0155,38   1981   Mama and Baby $600–$650

Limited to 8,000 USA. White tag, numbered, and boxed with certificate.

0151,32   1982   Richard Steiff Teddy $295–$350

Limited to 20,000. White tag, boxed, but without certificate. Replica from 1903.

0204,17   1982   Tea Party Set $425–$450

Limited to 10,000. White tag and boxed with certificate.

0203,00   1982   Original Teddy Set (white) $550–$575

Limited to 2,000. White tag and boxed.

0210,22   1983   Teddy Roosevelt Commemorative Set $275

Also called the Nimrod or Campfire Set. Limited to 10,000. Boxed and numbered. Some sets were sent back to Germany and the bears were undressed and retagged with yellow tags.

06160   1983   Margaret Strong Chocolate Set

Limited to 2,000. White ear tags. Originally sold as a boxed set but are now sold individually.

0118,25   1983   Boxer $95 up

Limited to 2,000.

0112,17   1983   Tiger (limited to 2,000) $95–$135
0112,28   1983   Tiger (limited to 2,000) $165–$185

0130,17   1983   Unicorn (limited to 2,000) $125
0130,27   1983   Unicorn (limited to 1,000) $175

0082,20   1984   "Roly-Poly" Circus Bear $80–$110

Museum Series piece. Limited to 9,000. Boxed and has a button only.

0080,08   1984   Felt Elephant $60–$75

Museum Series piece. Limited to 10,000. Boxed and has a button only.

Papa Bear (1980) and Mama and Baby Bears (1981). Because they are rare, these bears have become highly collectible.

A 13″ Santa Claus was issued in 1984; a 9″ Santa was issued in 1985.

A gray Richard Steiff bear issued in 1982 from the 1903 bear.

Dicky Bear (1985) is a replica of a bear made in 1930.

ITEM NUMBER	YEAR	NAME	PRICE

162,000 1984 Mama and Baby Giengen Set **$285–$310**
Limited to 16,000. Mama is 35 cm and baby is 10 cm. White ear tags and boxed.

4003 1984 Goldilocks and the Three Bears **$650–$750**
Limited to 2,000. The bears have white ear tags. Goldilocks, 16″; Papa Bear, 13½″; Mama Bear, 12″; Baby Bear, 9½″.

7635,28 1984 Santa Claus (13″ tall) **$250–$350**
Limited to 1,200. Replica from 1955.

0156,00 1984 Margaret Strong Cinnamon Set **unavailable**
Limited to 2,000. Originally sold boxed but are now sold separately. White ear tags.

0111,22 1984 Lion (limited to 2,000) **$95–$135**
0111,35 1984 Lion (limited to 2,000) **$165–$185**
Both have yellow ear tags.

0134,22 1985 Niki Rabbit (limited to 3,500) **$145–$165**
0134,28 1985 Niki Rabbit (limited to 2,500) **$195–$210**
Replica of 1952 rabbit with yellow ear tags.

4004 1985 Goldilocks and the Three Bears **$400–$525**
Limited to 5,000. Bears have white ear tags. Boxed and numbered. Goldilocks, 8″; Papa Bear, 9″; Mama Bear, 7″; Baby Bear, 5″.

0172,32 1985 Dicky Bear **$125–$150**
Limited to 20,000. White ear tag and boxed with certificate. Replica of 1930 bear.

7635,19 1985 Santa Claus (9″ tall) **$150–$165**
Produced in limited quantity and no longer available.

0085,12 1985 Bear on Wheels **$120–$145**
Museum Series piece. Limited to 12,000. Boxed and has a button only.

0105,17 1985 Penguin **$95–$135**
Museum Series piece. Limited to 8,000. Boxed and has a button only.

Teddy Clown (1986) is a replica of a bear made in 1926.

Muzzle Bear (1988) is a replica of a bear made in 1908. A larger size was available for a short time by special order.

"Silvia" Doll (1987) with a Jackie Teddy replica (1987).

"Roly-Poly" Bear was issued in 1988 in an edition of 3,000.

ITEM NUMBER	YEAR	NAME	PRICE
0158,21	1985	Margaret Strong White Bear with Leather Paws	**$125–135**
0158,31	1985	Margaret Strong White Bear with Leather Paws	**$185–215**
0158,41	1985	Margaret Strong White Bear with Leather Paws	**$225–295**

Limited to 2,000 each. White ear tags.

0170,32	1986	Teddy Clown	**$245–$265**

Limited to 5,000. White tag, comes with certificate. Replica of 1926 bear.

0101,14	1986	Bully Dog	**$120–$135**

Museum Series piece. Limited to 6,000. Boxed and has a button only.

0104,19	1986	Tabby Cat	**$120–$135**

Museum Series piece. Limited to 6,000. Boxed and has a button only.

0158,50	1986	Margaret Strong White Bear with Leather Paws	**$850 up**

Limited to 750. White ear tag and no box or number.

0100,86	1986	Elephant and Calliope	**$600–750**

Limited to 5,000. White tag and boxed with certificate. This is the first piece to the circus wagon, a five-piece series.

0190,25	1987	Jackie Bear	**$150–$165**

Limited to 10,000. White ear tag and boxed with certificate. Replica of 1953 bear.

0163,19	1987	Teddy Clown Junior	**$115**

Limited to 3,000 with white tags; 2,000 with yellow tags.

0171,41	1987	Teddy Rose	**$300–$350**

Limited to 10,000. White ear tag and boxed with certificate. Replica of 1925 bear.

0164,31	1987	Yellow Circus Dolly Bear	**$175**
0164,32	1987	Green Circus Dolly Bear	**$175**
0164,33	1987	Violet Circus Dolly Bear	**$175**

Limited to 2,000 each. White ear tags.

0090,11	1987	Polar Bear	**$95–$135**

Museum Series piece. Limited to 3,900. Boxed and has button only.

This bear comes with its own passport.

Mohair teddy bear wearing lederhosen, c. 1986.

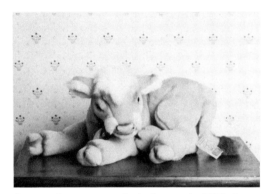

An acrylic cow made in the early 1980s is no longer available.

Baby Soft Jointed Teddies were introduced in 1987 but have been discontinued.

"Wigwag" Bear Pull Toy (1988) is a replica of a toy made in 1924.

ITEM NUMBER	YEAR	NAME	PRICE
9100,45	1987	Tennis Lady Doll	**$350**
9102,50	1987	Gentleman in Morning Coat Doll	**$300**
9112,45	1987	Peasant Man	**$375**
9110,43	1987	Peasant Lady	**$450**

Felt dolls with center seam on face. Limited to 2,000 each. Replicas of 1913 dolls.

0100,87	1987	Lion's Cage	**$275–$325**

Second piece of the circus wagon set. Limited to 5,000. Boxed with certificate.

0131,00	1987	Three Bears in a Tub	**$275**

Limited to 2,000 worldwide, 1,800 USA. White ear tags and boxed.

0120,19	1988	Bear Bandmaster	**$125–$135**
0120,19	1988	Dog Bandsman	**$125**
0122,19	1988	Cat Bandsman	**$125**
0123,19	1988	Lion Bandsman	**$125**
0134,19	1988	Crocodile Bandsman	**$125**

Limited to 5,000. All animals have white ear tags and come boxed.

0174,46	1988	Muzzle Bear	**$375–$400**

Replica of 1908 bear purchased by Richard Wright at record price. Limited to 5,000. White ear tag and boxed with certificate.

0115,18	1988	"Roly-Poly" Bear	**$125**
0116,28	1988	"Roly-Poly" Clown	**$250**

Both limited to 3,000 and have white ear tags. Replica of a 1908 bear and a 1908 clown.

0081,14	1988	Duck	**$125**

Museum Series piece. Limited to 4,000. Boxed and has button only.

0095,17	1988	Rabbit	**$145–$165**

Museum Series piece. Limited to 4,000. Boxed and has button only.

0173,40	1988	Black Bear	**$300–$325**

Limited to 4,000. White ear tag and boxed with certificate. Replica of 1907 bear.

0132,24	1988	"Wigwag" Bear Pull Toy	**$260**

Museum Series piece. Limited to 4,000. White tag and boxed. Replica of a 1924 toy.

ITEM NUMBER	YEAR	NAME	PRICE
0125,24	1988	Jumbo Elephant	**$300**
0126,20	1988	Donkey	**$185**

Limited to 3,000 with white tags. Both are mechanical. Replicas of a 1932 elephant and a 1931 donkey.

0190,35	1988	Jackie Bear (large)	**$300**

Limited to 4,000. White ear tag and boxed with certificate.

9130,43	1988	Coloro Clown Doll	**$500**

Limited to 3,000. Button in ear and tag on suit. Replica from 1911.

In addition to the above Limited Editions, many other items fall into the collectors' item category. The Margaret Strong Bears, which are replicas of 1904 bears, are made in many sizes and colors. The 1909 gold replicas were also made in several styles but have been discontinued. Giengen bears, made in gold and gray, are quite collectible. The 10- and 14-centimeter original jointed teddies have been discontinued.

The 1930 replica Teddy Baby may soon be discontinued, and the replica of the 1938 has been discontinued. Ophelia is not a limited edition but is collectible. The same is true of the Passport Bear, which comes with its own passport. The Berlin Bear from 1985 has been discontinued, as have the Luv Bear and the Buddha Bear. The Schnuffy Bear and the Clifford Berryman Bear are open stock, and some of the various combinations of fairy-tale dolls are limited. Many items in the regular line have also been discontinued over the years, which makes them very collectible.

Another recent Steiff offering deserves special mention. It is the line of new dolls that the company began producing in 1987. Called the "Margarete Steiff Doll," these new creations have fabric bodies with limbs that move and heads that nod and turn. They have hand-painted faces and real hair on a synthetic head. The clothes and accessories are produced from expensive materials that give the dolls a lifelike appearance. Twelve different models were produced the first year: "Silvia," "Margit," "Betina," "Piroschka," "Mimmi," "Bernd," "Gabi," "Babette," "Andrea," "Annette," "Andreas," and "Ulla."

The dolls come in a special box with a certificate and should become collectors' items in the near future because the Steiff Company plans to come out with new dolls each year and discontinue the earlier models.

Illustrated Price Guide to Steiff Toys

Every book on antiques and collectibles should have a price guide for collectors to refer to for approximate values of specific items. As anyone knows who is involved with the market, prices vary with the demand and with the circumstances under which the items are sold. Consequently, it is difficult to put an exact price on anything.

The following prices are to be viewed only as guidelines as to what someone might have paid or will pay for various items. Please don't assume that you can obtain that amount for all Steiff pieces or that a piece might not be worth more. A price is only valid if you have a customer who will pay that amount for it.

In the case of teddy bears, which are the hottest Steiff items, prices depend on the age, color, type of material used, how they are made, and whether they have buttons. For instance, the elephant button is considered the earliest, white is the most desirable color (or black, if any are available), long mohair is rarer than short, and the bears with center seams are in demand. The final requisite is appeal. Bears with cuter faces command higher prices than others. Rabbits and lambs are more popular than some other animals, but rare items such as the dinosaur and bat also bring high prices.

As with the Steiff at Auction section, descriptions are as complete as possible. In some cases the information on size or buttons, for example, is not available. Dates are also approximate since many items were made for many years after first being introduced.

Keep in mind that the rarity of an item increases the price even though certain pieces may not be as old as others of lesser value, and personal appeal is important. Also remember that prices can change drastically in a short time. This is especially true of the Collectors' Items, whose values will undoubtedly be different by the time this book is published.

White mohair teddy with glass eyes, 12" high (Courtesy Dee Hockenberry), **$1,200 up.**

Gold mohair teddy, 14" high, c. 1908 (Courtesy Barbara Lauver), **$2,500 up.**

Tan mohair teddy, 16½" high, with button, c. 1960, **$200 up.**

Faded pink mohair teddy, 13" high, with button, c. 1930, hat and ruff added (Courtesy Dee Hockenberry), **$1,000 up.**

Gold rayon plush teddy with button, 13" high, c. 1948, **$500 up.**

Curly mohair Zotties with buttons, 6", 8", 11", and 20" high, c. 1953, **$150, $250, $350,** and **$500 up.**

Mohair teddy with center seam, 20" high, c. 1905 (Courtesy Dee Hockenberry), **$3,000 up.**

Mohair Zotty with button, 30" high, 1955, **$1,000 up.**

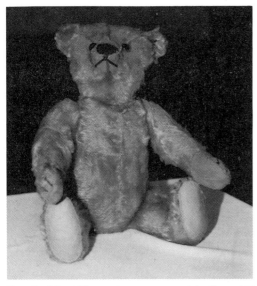

Tan teddy with center seam and button, 16"
high, c. 1905, pads replaced (Courtesy Bunny
Walker), **$2,000 up.**

Gold mohair teddy with button, 8" high, c. 1904
(Courtesy Bunny Walker), **$1,200 up.**

Beige mohair teddy, 16" high, c. 1907, mint condition except worn spot behind ear (Courtesy
Bunny Walker), **$3,000 up.**

Cinnamon mohair teddy, 10" high, c. 1908, mint
condition (Courtesy Bunny Walker), **$1,500 up.**

White mohair teddy with button, 16" high, with small patch on right paw, c. 1912 (Courtesy Barbara Lauver), **$2,500 up.**

Gold cotton plush Teddy Baby, 8½" high, c. 1948, **$500 up.**

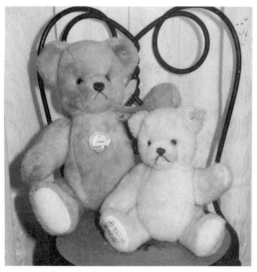

Dralon "Petseys" with soft stuffing, c. 1970s (Courtesy Pamela Elkins). *Left,* 12" high, **$150;** *right,* 9" high, **$75.**

Brown mohair Teddy Baby, 12" high, c. 1950, **$800 up.**

Brown curly mohair Teddy Baby with original collar and bell, 5' high, c. 1950, rare (Courtesy Dottie Ayers), **$5,500 up.**

Tan mohair teddy with glass eyes and button, 48" high, c. 1910 (Courtesy Barbara Lauver), **$10,000 up.**

Left: Tan mohair teddy, 16" high, with some wear and patches, *ff* button, pre-1910, **$1,350 up.** *Right:* Tan mohair teddy, 9½" high, with some wear, c. 1906, (Courtesy Dee Hockenberry), **$850 up.**

1982 reproduction of a 12" Margaret Strong bear with a gold mohair teddy with button, 11¾" high, c. 1907 (Courtesy Dee Hockenberry), **$1,200 up.**

Assortment of Steiff teddies, all c. 1906–10, except small rattle bear in front, c. 1920 (Courtesy Sue Potchen), **$500–$2,000 up.**

Gold mohair teddy, 28″ high, with patches, c. 1908 (Courtesy Barbara Lauver), **$7,500 up.**

Brown mohair teddy, 24″ high, c. 1906, **$5,000 up,** and small Niki rabbit, c. 1950 (Courtesy Barbara Lauver), **$250 up.**

Gold mohair teddy, 24" high, c. 1920 (Courtesy Barbara Lauver), **$5,000 up.**

Tan mohair teddy, 20" high, c. 1950, **$1,500 up,** and fully jointed pink pig, c. 1913, **$600 up** (Courtesy Barbara Lauver).

White mohair teddy with blank button, 16" high, c. 1905 (Courtesy Barbara Lauver), **$3,000 up.**

Tan mohair teddy with center seam, 20" high, mint condition (Courtesy Dee Hockenberry), **$4,000 up.**

Three 16″ mohair teddies in various colors with center seams, c. 1907–12 (Courtesy Barbara Lauver), each **$2,000 up.**

Left: Beige mohair teddy, 24″ high, c. 1907, **$5,000 up.** *Right:* Gold mohair teddy, 24″ high, c. 1920, **$4,000 up** (Courtesy Barbara Lauver).

Stairstep assortment of old teddies, 5″ to 30″ high, c. 1905–10 (Courtesy Sue Potchen), **$300–$7,000.**

Two white mohair teddies, 20″ high, c. 1907 (Courtesy Barbara Lauver), each **$4,000 up.**

Gray mohair teddy, 18″ high, c. 1910, **$2,500 up.**

Brown mohair bear with growler, 27″ by 19″, c. 1908, wheels missing, mint condition (Courtesy Sue Potchen), **$1,000 up.**

Beige mohair teddy, 18″ high, with button, c. 1940, **$1,000 up.**

Brown mohair teddy with squeaker, 13″ high, c. 1915, rare (Courtesy Dee Hockenberry), **$1,200 up.**

White curly mohair teddy, 20" high, c. 1906 (Courtesy Barbara Lauver), **$4,000 up.**

Beige mohair teddy (with photo), 24" high, c. 1906 (Courtesy Barbara Lauver), **$6,000 up.**

Beige mohair teddy, 28" high, c. 1908 (Courtesy Barbara Lauver), **$8,000 up.**

Beige mohair teddy, 20" high, c. 1907, with patches (Courtesy Barbara Lauver), **$3,500 up.**

Two gold mohair teddies, 28" high, c. 1908–10 (Courtesy Barbara Lauver), both **$8,000 up.**

Gold mohair teddy, 16" high, c. 1920 (Courtesy Barbara Lauver), **$2,500 up.**

Top left: White mohair teddy, 16" high, with blank button, c. 1905, **$2,500 up.** *Top right:* Honey teddy with center seam, 23" high, c. 1905, **$5,000 up.** *Bottom left:* Tumbler teddy, 12" high, c. 1915, **$1,500 up,** and rod bear, 20" high, c. 1902, **$5,000 up** (Courtesy Barbara Lauver).

Cinnamon mohair teddy, 20" high, c. 1907 (Courtesy Barbara Lauver), **$4,000 up.**

Beige mohair teddy, 12" high, c. 1912 (Courtesy Barbara Lauver), **$1,500 up.**

Felt tea cosy, c. 1908, **$800 up.**

Dralon cozy teddy, jointed; plastic eyes; 23" high, c. 1960s, **$200 up.**

Felt Dutch girl doll, 12" high, **$800 up,** with 5" bear, **$350 up,** both c. 1913 (Courtesy Barbara Lauver).

Beige mohair teddy with button, 28″ high, c. 1908, excellent condition (Courtesy Sue Potchen), **$8,000 up.**

Felt boy doll, 8" high, c. 1913, **$600 up.**

Felt girl doll, 8" high, c. 1913, **$600 up.**

Velvet Mickey Mouse with felt ears, 7" high, eyes and whiskers replaced, rare (Courtesy Dee Hockenberry), **$575 up.**

Musical Santa, "Musicanto," plays "Jingle Bells," c. 1950s, rare, **$1,500 up.**

Policeman doll, 10" high, head made by Steiff, body and mechanism by Shuco, mint condition (Courtesy Harriet Purtill), **$1,200 up.**

Mohair Pekinese ("Peky") with jointed head, $3\frac{1}{2}$" high, c. 1950s, **$50 up.**

Felt policeman doll, c. 1913, **$1,000 up.**

Long mohair Wolfhound, 8" high, c. 1934, rare, **$350 up.**

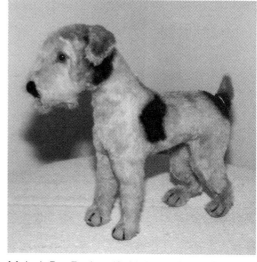

Mohair "Musicanto" Cockie, 5½" high; music plays when tail is turned; button and red tag, c. 1950, rare (Courtesy Dottie Ayers), **$550 up.**

Mohair Fox Terrier, 6½" high, c. 1940s (Courtesy Jane Viprino), **$75 up.**

Mohair Airedale, 6½" high, c. 1950 (Courtesy Jane Viprino), **$75 up.**

Felt and long mohair Kitty with elephant button, 7½" high, c. 1908, rare (Courtesy Dottie Ayers), **$1,500 up.**

Mohair "Biggie" Beagle, 4½" high, with button, c. 1950, **$50 up.**

Mohair "Bully" with leather collar, 4" high, c. 1950s, **$50 up.**

Mohair "Molly" dog, 6" high, with old chest tag, c. 1930 (Courtesy Dee Hockenberry), **$50 up.**

"Molly" Dog, seated, with ribbon and belt, 4" high, with button, c. 1950s, **$50 up.**

St. Bernard pup with original collar, 8" high, c. 1950s, somewhat rare (Courtesy Dee Hockenberry), **$180 up.**

Velvet Dachshund on iron wheels, 6" high, with *ff* button, c. 1915, mint condition (Courtesy Harriet Purtill), **$900 up.**

Wool plush Chow dog, 5" high, c. 1950s, rare, **$100.**

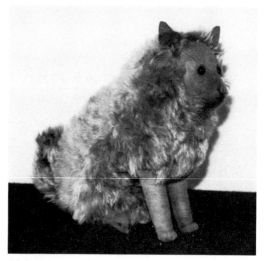

Mohair and felt Pomeranian, 8" high, c. 1913, rare (Courtesy Barbara Lauver), **$800 up.**

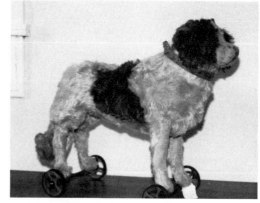

Large mohair St. Bernard on iron wheels, c. 1913 (Courtesy Barbara Lauver), **$500 up.**

Brown and white mohair Cocker Spaniel with jointed head, 7" high, tiny *ff* button, mint condition (Courtesy Barbara Sykora), **$250.**

Tan, gray, and white wool Fox Terrier on wooden wheels, 11½" high, with chest tag and *ff* button (Courtesy Barbara Sykora), **$250 up.**

Rust and white mohair "Bully," 10" high, with tiny *ff* buttons on ear and collar, blank button on leash, c. 1930s, mint condition, rare (Courtesy Barbara Sykora), **$950 up.**

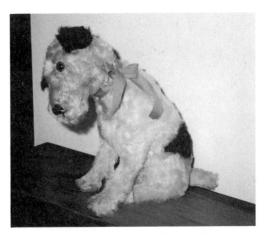

Black and white mohair Fox Terrier with jointed head and glass eyes, 12" high, with *ff* button (Courtesy Barbara Sykora), **$300 up.**

Black and white mohair "Bully" on wooden wheels, with jointed head and glass eyes, 10½" high, *ff* button, excellent condition, rare (Courtesy Barbara Sykora), **$1,000 up.**

Mohair "Gussy" Kitten with button, 5" high, c. 1950s, **$50 up.**

Gray and white mohair hand puppet, 8½" high, c. 1950s, **$50 up.**

Gray and white cotton plush kitten with original bell and ribbon, 4" high, gray painted blank button, c. 1940s (Courtesy Harriet Purtill), **$225.**

Early black and white Cocker Spaniel hand puppet with glass eyes and tiny *ff* button (Courtesy Barbara Sykora), **$175 up.**

Studio-size mohair rabbit, jointed, c. 1950s, **$500 up.**

Mohair "Record Rabbit" on wooden wheels, with button, c. 1950 (Courtesy Barbara Lauver), **$400 up.**

Boy on pumper cart with wooden wheels, c. 1926, rare (Courtesy Barbara Lauver), **$500 up.**

Velveteen "Roly-Poly" rabbit, c. 1913, rare (Courtesy Barbara Lauver), **$500 up.**

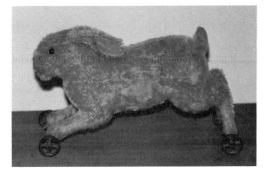

Mohair running rabbit on iron wheels, c. 1913 (Courtesy Barbara Lauver), **$500 up.**

Mohair "Tucky" Turkey with felt and metal legs, 4" high, with button, c. 1950s, **$100 up.**

Velvet squirrel with pewter button, $2\frac{1}{2}$" high, c. 1940s, unusual, **$65 up.**

Mohair goose with swivel head, 12" high, c. 1913 (Courtesy Dee Hockenberry), **$350 up.**

Floppy hen with button and chest tag, 5" high, c. 1950s, unusual (Courtesy Dee Hockenberry), **$110 up.**

Mohair chickens with felt trim, small ones with metal legs, c. 1950s. Large, **$75 up**; small, **$50 up**.

Bird Wedding with wool miniature birds dressed and mounted on board, with pewter buttons, c. 1940s, **$150 up**.

Mohair lion cub, 8" high, with old *ff* button, c. 1925 (Courtesy Dee Hockenberry), **$200 up**.

"Tysus" Dinosaur with jointed arms, 17" high, c. 1960s (Courtesy Dee Hockenberry), **$1,500 up**.

Mohair tiger cub, jointed, 4½" high, c. 1950s, mint condition (Courtesy Dee Hockenberry), **$125 up**.

Mohair running tigers, 11" and 7" high, c. 1950s. Left, **$75**; right, **$50**.

Long and short mohair llama with button, 6" high, c. 1960s, **$75 up.**

Long mohair "Gaty" Alligator with felt trim, 13" long, with button, c. 1950s, **$75 up.**

Wool plush lion cub, jointed head, button, c. 1950s, **$50 up.**

Mohair boar with blue glass eyes, 4" high, with button, c. 1950s, **$65 up.**

Mohair rhino with plastic eyes, 4" high, c. 1950s, **$50 up.**

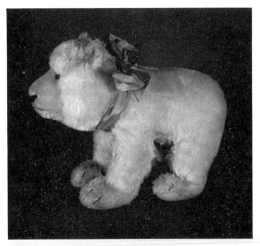

Polar bear with blue glass eyes, 8½" by 11", c. 1950s, mint condition (Courtesy Dee Hockenberry), **$300 up.**

Long white "Wiggy" Weasel with Dralon pipe-cleaner tail, 8" high, c. 1960s, **$75 up.**

Mohair baby goat with felt horns, 6" high, with button, c. 1950s, **$50 up.**

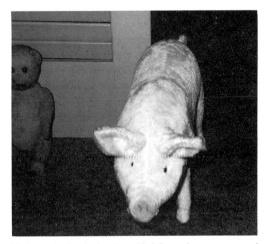

Pink mohair plush pig with blue glass eyes and squeaker, 8½" by 13", with pewter button, c. 1925, **$600 up.**

Mohair "Spidy" Spider, 4½", c. 1960s, **$300 up.**

Large "Lupy" Wolf, long mohair with felt tongue, c. 1960s, **$500 up.**

Mohair "Bessy" Cow with felt trim, plastic eyes, and brass bell on leather collar, 6" high, c. 1960s, mint condition, **$200 up.**

Long "Super Molly" Lion Cub, acrylic with foam stuffing, 20" long, with button, c. 1987, **$380.**

Mohair ox with plastic eyes and leather collar with bell, 4" high, c. 1960s, **$75 up.**

Velvet donkey with red checkered pack and plastic eyes, 5½" high, c. 1960s, **$50 up.**

Mohair panda, 4" high, with chest tag and button, c. 1950s, mint condition (Courtesy Harriet Purtill), **$325 up.**

Long mohair camel on iron wheels, c. 1913, mint condition (Courtesy Barbara Lauver), **$800 up.**

Mohair moose with felt antlers, 12½" and 5" high, c. 1960s (Courtesy Jane Viprino). Left, **$150 up;** right, **$75 up.**

Curly and short mohair sheep on iron wheels, c. 1913, rare (Courtesy Barbara Lauver), **$600 up.**

Large velvet dangling frog, unjointed, c. 1960s, **$350 up.**

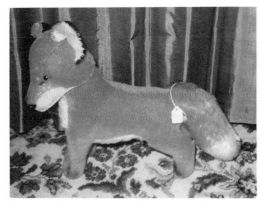

Long red with white mohair fox, 12" long, unusual (Courtesy Barbara Lauver), **$600 up.**

Left: Black and white mohair "Lambys" with ribbons and bells, 12" and 8" high, **$100** and **$75**. *Right:* "Swapls," 8" and 5" high, **$75** and **$50** (Courtesy Jane Viprino).

Pink mohair pig, unjointed, clothes added, 13" high, c. 1930s, **$300 up.**

Multicolor long mohair parrot, 5½" high, with button, c. 1960s, **$50 up.**

Large brown mohair bear on wooden wheels, c. 1920s (Courtesy Barbara Lauver), **$800 up.**

"Lucki" Dwarf with felt body and clothes, rubber head, leather shoes, and jointed arms, 5" high, c. 1950s, **$50 up.**

Swingful of Niki bunnies from the 1950s, except velveteen bunny, c. 1908. Niki 8", **$200 up;** Niki 9", **$250 up;** Niki 11", **$350 up;** velveteen, **$500 up.**

Steiff Catalogues: 1955, 1957, 1959, 1960

 Catalogue pages in this book begin with 1955, showing all new pages that were not included in the book *Steiff Teddy Bears, Dolls, and Toys.* Segments from the 1954–55 catalogue were printed in that book, but the 1955 catalogue shows some new items that did not appear.

Since the 1950s were such important years for Steiff, especially in the United States, many examples from this period are available to collectors today. This was also the time when Steiff came out with a line of miniatures, which were less expensive to collect and easier to display. Many new hand puppets were also added each year, and the "cosy" animals were introduced.

Animals that had been in the line before appear in different sizes and positions from year to year, so it is difficult to pick out each new item unless it is marked as being new. I have included as many pages from these catalogues as possible so that readers can compare the numbers with the animals.

Some of the new items appearing in the 1955 catalogue are a standing panda, "Goldy" Hamster in two sizes, "Slo" Turtle, a green frog, birds with movable wings called "Fink" and "Maise," "Wittie" Owl in two sizes, "Quaggy" Duck, and "Teddy II." A hippo, rhino, seal, and koala appear for

the first time, as well as a schnauzer and "Joggie" Hedgehog.

In the 1957 catalogue one finds for the first time "Xorry" Fox, a llama, "Mungo" Ape, "Raccy" Raccoon, a crocodile, "Rennie" Reindeer, and a black Persian lamb.

The 1959 new items are "Paddy" Walrus, "Piccy" Pelican, "Sigi" Sea Horse, "Revue Susi" Cocker Spaniel,

"Diggy" Badger, "Perri" Squirrel, "Lizzy" Lizard, "Topsy" Cat, Cosy Siamy Cat, Floppy Beagle, Floppy Poodle, "Flack," "Bluebonnet," and "Bullfinch" Birds, a miniature poodle, a seated tiger, an 11-inch multicolor frog, and the mountain lamb, which was later called "Snucki."

The 1960 catalogue, which does not include numbers, shows for the first time the Okapi, "Biggie" Beagle, "Trampy" Elephant, and "Nagy" Beaver.

75 Jahre
Steiff Knopf im Ohr

Das erste weichgestopfte Tier der Welt, ein kleiner Elefant, wurde vor 75 Jahren von Margarete Steiff geschaffen. Es war ein Geschenk an ihre kleinen Neffen, die sofort hell begeistert waren. Sie hatte damit instinktiv ein prachtvolles neues Spielzeug erfunden, unzerbrechlich, weich und kindlich.

Die Idee dieser entzückenden Spielkameraden ist heute zu einer großartigen Spitzenleistung entwickelt. Jedes Tier ist eine köstliche Nachbildung der Natur. Mit großer Liebe und von vielen geschulten Händen werden Steiff-Tiere in Handarbeit hergestellt. Sie sind nicht nur naturgetreu, sondern unverwüstlich im Gebrauch, bei braven wie auch wilden Kindern, mit denen junge Tiere viel Gemeinsames haben – die runden Formen, den weichen Körper und den gutartigen Ausdruck.

Steiff-Tiere bringen den Zoo zum Kind, das ganze Tierreich mit allen markanten Tieren. Wie schön, wenn wilde und zahme Tiere friedlich eine Beziehung zum Kinde finden und Freunde werden für die lange glückliche Kindheit, als ein letzter Rest des Paradieses. Diese erste Begegnung mit dem Tier, im frühesten Alter, vermittelt nachhaltige Eindrücke – ein Grund mehr, nur das Schönste zu wählen, eine Sammlung der lebensechten Tiere von

Knopf im Ohr

Größenbezeichnung: Die letzten beiden Ziffern jeder Nummer bedeuten Kopfhöhe in cm. Soweit nichts anderes vermerkt, sind alle Tiere aus feinstem, glänzendem Mohairplüsch. Preisänderungen vorbehalten.

Leopard
48 a / 2317,1 14.80
      2328,1 25.—
      2343,1 62.50
      2360,1 119.—

Clownie
88 / 743 25.—

Tiger
70/2317,1 14.80
    2328,1 25.—
    2343,1 62.50
    2360,1 119.—

Mähnen-Löwe
48/2335,1 33.50

Panda	Goldhamster „Goldy"		Schildkröte „Slo"		Gucki	Fink		Eule „Wittie"		Meise	
12 P/1312,0 6.50	4310	5.50	2310	6.50	718,1 11.—	1312,3	6.50	4310	6.50	1312,4	6.50
	4314	7.50	2314	8.80		1317,3	10.50	4314	8.80	1317,4	10.50

Quaggy	Nilpferd		Pinguin		Nashorn		Teddyli	Seehund	
22/712 5.80	1310,0	6.50	4310	4.50	1310,0	6.50	12/712 5.80	4310	6.50
	1314,0	9.20	4314	5.80	1314,0	9.20		4314	8.80 3
			4322	10.50					

Steiff

A Koala		B Schimpanse			C Zotty Bär		
4312	7.20						
5322	13.90	5325	10.50	5350,2 39.–	6317,1	10.50	6328,1 22.–
5335,2 29.–		5335	17.50	5360,2 55.–	6322,1	13.50	6335,1 31.50

Der Original Steiff Teddy

				Weich-Elefant	Weich-Bär	Panda-Bär 5322	12.–
5322	8.50	5335,2	15.–			5328,2	17.50
5325,2	10.50	5343,2	25.–	4322,1 19.50	4322,1 17.50	5335,2	26.–
5328,2	12.50	5350,2	37.50				

4	Jackie 5317	8.90	Coco (Pavian)	Teddy Baby 7322,2	11.80	Eisbär	Braunbär
	5325	13.50	5335 29.50	7328,2	17.50	1317,02 11.50	1317,02 11.50
	5335	24.50		7340,2	33.–	1325,02 19.50	1325,02 24.–

Cockie Spaniel
29/2335,1 32.50

Snobby Pudel (gegliedert)
grau oder weiß oder schwarz
58/5314 8.80   5335,2 32.50
5322 15.50   5343,2 48.50

Snobby Pudel
grau oder schwarz
58/2335,1 32.50

Pekinese	1310,0	7.20	Waldi	1317,02	13.50	Mecki		Schnauzer	1314,0	9.80	Hexie	1309,0	6.50
	1314,0	11.—		1322,02	21.50	(Cop.Diehl Film)			1322,0	16.80		1313,0	10.90
	1322,02	22.50		1328,02	34.—	728 B	20.50						

Boxer		Cockie	3314	10.50	Bully	1317,0	11.50	Rehbock	1335,0	17.80	St. Claus		Reh	1328,0	15.50
3314	9.80		3317	14.50		1322,02	17.—				731	21.50			
			3322,2	21.—											

5

Foxterrier
1317,0   9.80
1322,0   12.50
1328,02   18.50
1335,02   30. —

Kitty Katze
5317   14.50
5322,2   21. —

Fiffy Katze
2312   6.95
2317   10.50
2325,1   20.50

Zwerg Lucki   718,2   11. —
730,2   19.80
755,2   62. —

Kater   7410   5.20
7314   8. —
7317   9.50
7322   13. —

Gussy Katze
6312,0   6.50
6317,0   11.50

Tabby Katze
1310,0   4.80
1314,0   8. —
1317,0   11.50

Lucki
713,2   6.50

Tabby
1310 ex   5.90
1314 ex   11.80
1317 ex   15.50

Susi
3314   8.80
3317   12. —
3322,2   14.80

Mecki   728 B   20.50
717 B   11. —

Joggi   4312   7.20

Ziege   6314,0   7.80
6322,0   12.50

Cockie   1310 ex   7.50

Ente   2311 ex   6.50

Bully   1310 ex   7.50

Lamm   6514,0   6.50
6522,0   11. —

6

Floppy Schlaftiere, superweich

E Floppy Lamm
7517 8.80 7528 17.—

F Floppy Hase
7317 9.80 7328 18.50

A	Floppy Panda	
	7317	9.80
	7328	18.50
B	Floppy Zotty	
	7317	9.80
	7328	18.50
C	Floppy Cockie	
	7317	9.80
	7328	18.50
D	Floppy Kitty	
	7317	9.80
	7328	18.50

Clownie	Elefant	Kamel	Esel	Niki	5322	13.50
719 11.50	6317,0 14.80	1528,0 15.80	1322,0 16.80		5328,2	17.50
	6322,01 19.80	1535,0 21.—	1328,0 21.50		5317	25.50

Pony	Record Peter	Baby Bär	Baby Hase		Reh	
1317,0 10.50	beim Ziehen Bewegung u.Stimme	7322 11.50	7322 11.50	6317,0 8.80	2314	6.50
	325 16.80	7330 18.50	7330 18.50	6322,0 11.50	2317	8.80

7

123

Plüsch-Miniaturen (auch für Sammler)

1 Clownie	714	6.50	6 Coco	1310,0	5.90	11 Teddy	5318	6.90	16 Bär	1312,0	6.50
2 Eisbär	1312,0	6.50	7 Teddy	5310	3.90	12 Eichhorn	4410	5.80	17 Teddy-Baby	7309	4.80
3 Jocko	5310	3.90	8 Teddy	5318	6.90	13 Nilpferd	1310,0	6.50	18 Seehund	4310	6.50
4 Panda	1312,0	6.50	9 Jocko	5310	3.90	14 Pinguin	4310	4.50	19 Jocko	5310	3.90
5 Rabe	1508	2 –	10 Nashorn	1310,0	6.50	15 Jocko	5310	3.90	20 Elefant	6310,0	6.50
									21 Kamel	1514,0	6.50

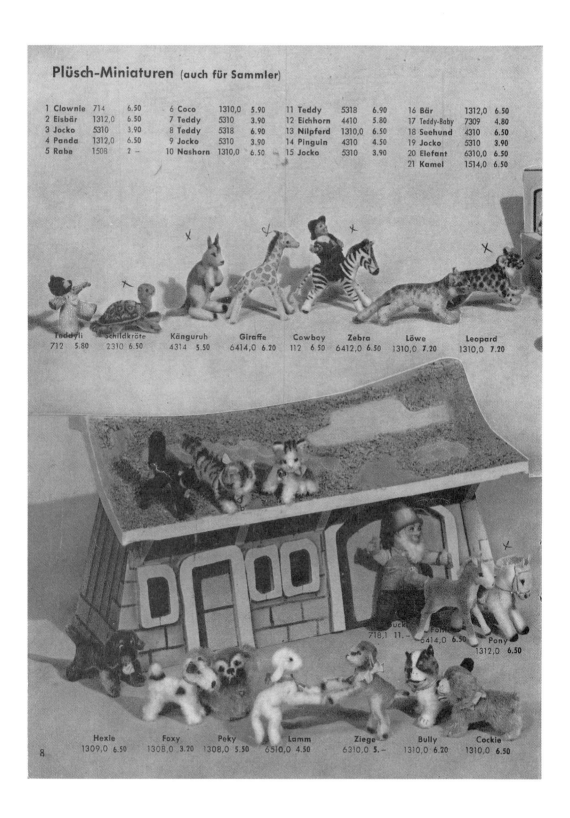

Teddyli 712 5.80 Schildkröte 2310 6.50 Känguruh 4314 5.50 Giraffe 6414,0 6.20 Cowboy 112 6.50 Zebra 6412,0 6.50 Löwe 1310,0 7.20 Leopard 1310,0 7.20

Bucki 718,1 11.– Fohlen 6414,0 6.50 Pony 1312,0 6.50

Hexie 1309,0 6.50 Foxy 1308,0 3.20 Peky 1308,0 5.50 Lamm 6510,0 4.50 Ziege 6310,0 5.– Bully 1310,0 6.20 Cockie 1310,0 6.50

8

a	Kater	7408	4.—	f	Bazi	3310	6.50	l	Gest. Kater	313 B	5.80
b	Tabby	1310,0	4.80	g	Molly	3310	4.80	m	Hahn	1310	3.30
c	Susi	3310	4.80	h	Cockie	3310	6.50	n	Boxer	3310	6.20
d	Uhu	4310	6.50	i	Schnauzer	1310,0	5.50	o	Boxer	1310,0	6.50
e	Esel	1412,0	6.50	k	Terry	1310,0	4.20	p	Frosch	3408	5.—

Schwein		Macki			Hasen				Bambi		Goldhamster	
1407,0 br	4.—	712 B	**6.20**	4310	4.80	3309	4.80	1308,0	4.80	(Walt Disney)		4310	5.50 q
1407,0 r	4.—									7414,0	6.50		

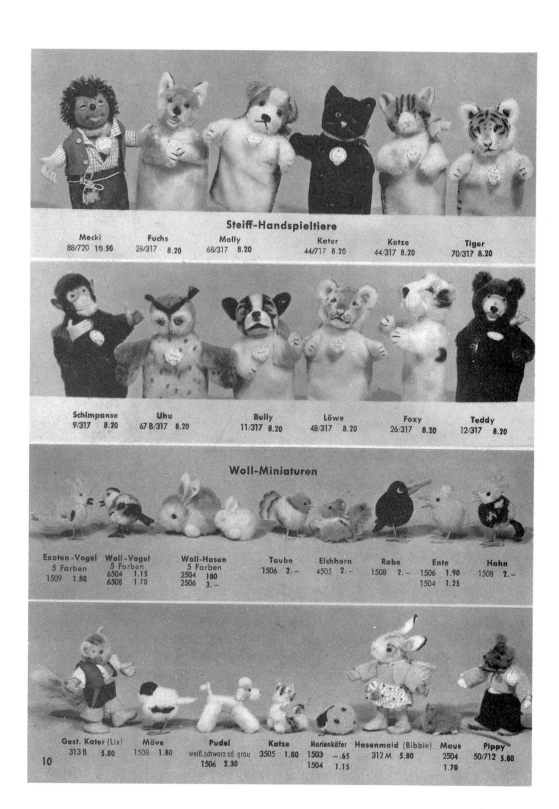

Steiff-Handspieltiere

Mecki	Fuchs	Molly	Kater	Katze	Tiger
88/720 19.50	28/317 8.20	68/317 8.20	44/717 8.20	44/317 8.20	70/317 8.20

Schimpanse	Uhu	Bully	Löwe	Foxy	Teddy
9/317 8.20	67 B/317 8.20	11/317 8.20	48/317 8.20	26/317 8.20	12/317 8.20

Woll-Miniaturen

Exoten-Vogel	Woll-Vogel	Woll-Hasen	Taube	Eichhorn	Rabe	Ente	Hahn
5 Farben	5 Farben	5 Farben	1506 2.-	4505 2.-	1508 2.-	1506 1.90	1508 2.-
1509 1.80	6504 1.15	2504 180				1504 1.25	
	6508 1.70	2506 3.-					

	Gest. Kater (Lix)	Möve	Pudel	Katze	Marienkäfer	Hasenmaid (Bibbie)	Maus	Pippy
10	313 B 5.80	1508 1.80	weiß, schwarz od. grau	3505 1.80	1503 -.65	312 M 5.80	2504	50/712 5.80
			1506 2.30		1504 1.15		1.70	

Mecki
(nach Diehl-Film)
Redaktions-Igel
der Jllustrierten Rundfunk-
Zeitung HÖR ZU.
Die populäre Märchenfigur,
die Helden vieler
Abenteuer

Macki	Micki	Mecki	Mucki
712 B 6.20	728 M 20.50	728 B 20.50	712 M 6.20
	717 M 11.—	717 B 11.—	

Cosy Waschtiere
mit Schaumgummi - Füllung
Fell aus dickem, unverwüst-
lichem Dralon - Plüsch. Sehr
weich und angenehm. Ver-
tragen Ganzwaschung und
Durchnässung (Badewanne)
jedoch nicht Kochen.

A Cosy Teddy	B Cosy Orsi	C Cosy Molly	D Cosy Mummy	E Cosy Kitty
12/5622 16.80	12/6620 16.80	68/6620 16.80	36/6620 16.80	44/6620 16.80

11

127

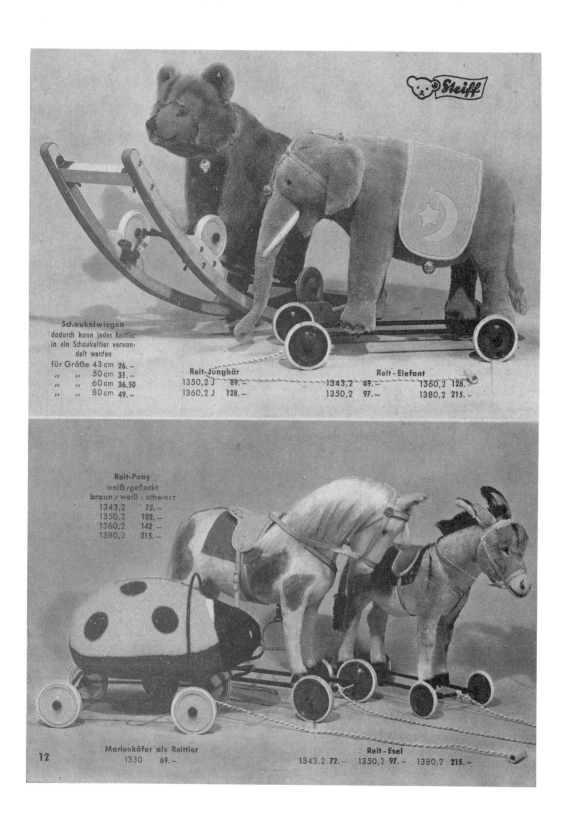

Schaukelwiegen
dadurch kann jedes Reittier
in ein Schaukeltier verwandelt werden

für Größe 43 cm	26. –
" " 50 cm	31. –
" " 60 cm	36.50
" " 80 cm	49. –

Reit-Jungbär		Reit-Elefant	
1350,2 J	89. –	1343,2	69. –	1360,2	128. –
1360,2 J	128. –	1350,2	97. –	1380,2	215. –

Reit-Pony
weiß/gefleckt
braun / weiß / schwarz

1343,2	75. –
1350,2	103. –
1360,2	142. –
1380,2	215. –

12

Marienkäfer als Reittier		Reit-Esel		
1330	69. –	1343,2 72. –	1350,2 97. –	1380,2 215. –

128

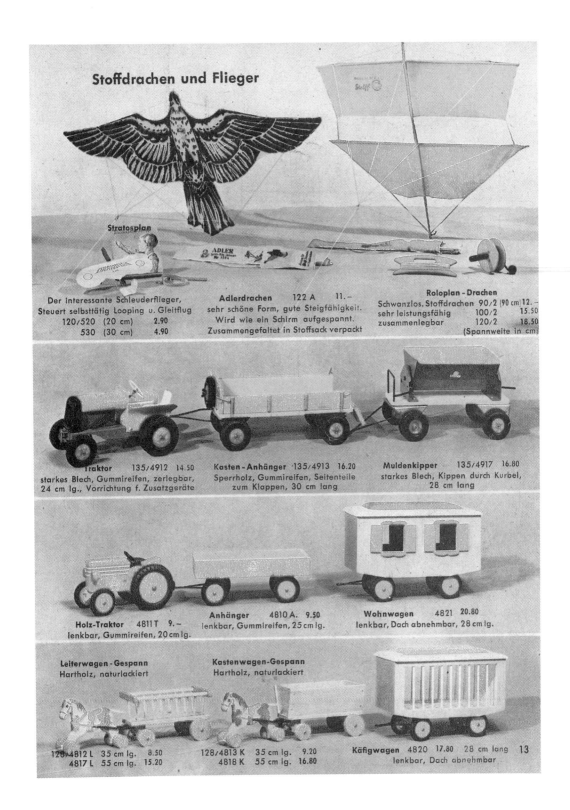

Stoffdrachen und Flieger

Stratosplan

Der interessante Schleuderflieger,
Steuert selbsttätig Looping u. Gleitflug
120/520 (20 cm)   2.90
530 (30 cm)   4.90

Adlerdrachen   122 A   11.–
sehr schöne Form, gute Steigfähigkeit.
Wird wie ein Schirm aufgespannt.
Zusammengefaltet in Stoffsack verpackt

Roloplan - Drachen
Schwanzlos. Stoffdrachen 90/2 (90 cm) 12.–
sehr leistungsfähig   100/2   15.50
zusammenlegbar   120/2   18.50
(Spannweite in cm)

Traktor   135/4912 14.50
starkes Blech, Gummireifen, zerlegbar,
24 cm lg., Vorrichtung f. Zusatzgeräte

Kasten - Anhänger 135/4913 16.20
Sperrholz, Gummireifen, Seitenteile
zum Klappen, 30 cm lang

Muldenkipper   135/4917 16.80
starkes Blech, Kippen durch Kurbel,
28 cm lang

Holz-Traktor   4811 T   9.–
lenkbar, Gummireifen, 20 cm lg.

Anhänger   4810 A. 9.50
lenkbar, Gummireifen, 25 cm lg.

Wohnwagen   4821 20.80
lenkbar, Dach abnehmbar, 28 cm lg.

Leiterwagen - Gespann
Hartholz, naturlackiert

128/4812 L   35 cm lg.   8.50
4817 L   55 cm lg.   15.20

Kastenwagen-Gespann
Hartholz, naturlackiert

128/4813 K   35 cm lg.   9.20
4818 K   55 cm lg.   16.80

Käfigwagen   4820 17.80   28 cm lang   13
lenkbar, Dach abnehmbar

129

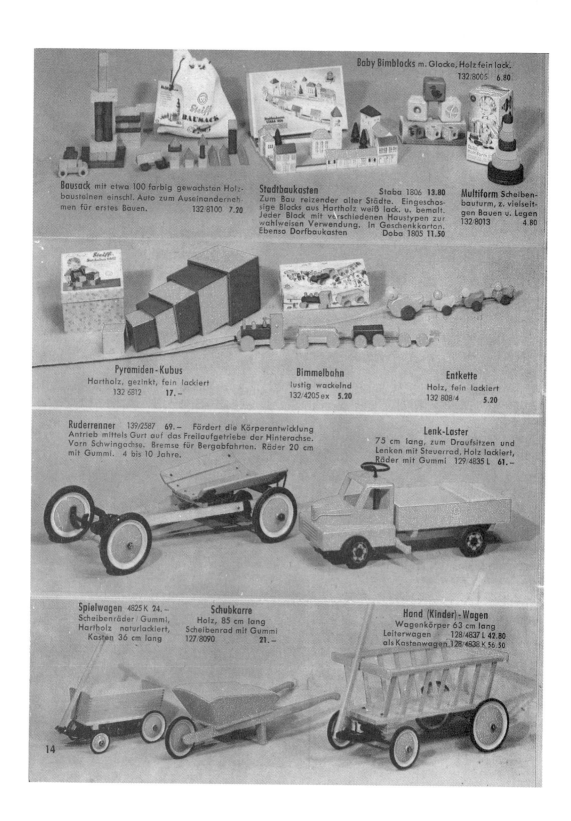

Baby Bimblocks m. Glocke, Holz fein lack.
132/8005 6.80

Bausack mit etwa 100 farbig gewachsten Holz-bausteinen einschl. Auto zum Auseinanderneh-men für erstes Bauen.   132/8100 **7.20**

Stadtbaukasten   Staba 1806 **13.80**
Zum Bau reizender alter Städte. Eingeschos-sige Blocks aus Hartholz weiß lack. u. bemalt. Jeder Block mit verschiedenen Haustypen zur wahlweisen Verwendung. In Geschenkkarton. Ebenso Dorfbaukasten   Doba 1805 **11.50**

Multiform Scheiben-bauturm, z. vielseiti-gen Bauen u. Legen
132/8013   **4.80**

Pyramiden-Kubus
Hartholz, gezinkt, fein lackiert
132 6812   **17.—**

Bimmelbahn
lustig wackelnd
132/4205 ex   **5.20**

Entkette
Holz, fein lackiert
132 808/4   **5.20**

Ruderrenner 139/2587 **69.—** Fördert die Körperentwicklung Antrieb mittels Gurt auf das Freilaufgetriebe der Hinterachse. Vorn Schwingachse. Bremse für Bergabfahrten. Räder 20 cm mit Gummi. 4 bis 10 Jahre.

Lenk-Laster
75 cm lang, zum Draufsitzen und Lenken mit Steuerrad, Holz lackiert, Räder mit Gummi 129/4835 L **61.—**

Spielwagen 4825 K **24.—**
Scheibenräder / Gummi, Hartholz naturlackiert, Kasten 36 cm lang

Schubkarre
Holz, 85 cm lang
Scheibenrad mit Gummi
127/8090   **21.—**

Hand (Kinder)-Wagen
Wagenkörper 63 cm lang
Leiterwagen 128/4837 L **42.80**
als Kastenwagen 128/4838 K 56.50

14

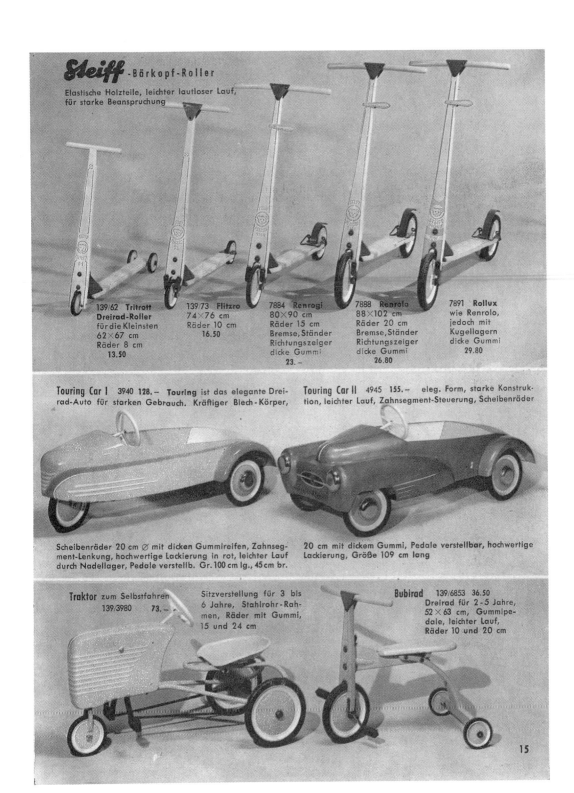

Steiff -Bärkopf-Roller

Elastische Holzteile, leichter lautloser Lauf, für starke Beanspruchung

139/62 Tritrott Dreirad-Roller für die Kleinsten 62×67 cm Räder 8 cm **13.50**

139/73 Flitzro 74×76 cm Räder 10 cm **16.50**

7884 Renrogi 80×90 cm Räder 15 cm Bremse, Ständer Richtungszeiger dicke Gummi **23.—**

7888 Renrolo 88×102 cm Räder 20 cm Bremse, Ständer Richtungszeiger dicke Gummi **26.80**

7891 Rollux wie Renrolo, jedoch mit Kugellagern dicke Gummi **29.80**

Touring Car I 3940 **128.— Touring** ist das elegante Dreirad-Auto für starken Gebrauch. Kräftiger Blech-Körper,

Scheibenräder 20 cm ∅ mit dicken Gummireifen, Zahnsegment-Lenkung, hochwertige Lackierung in rot, leichter Lauf durch Nadellager, Pedale verstellb. Gr. 100 cm lg., 45 cm br.

Touring Car II 4945 **155.—** eleg. Form, starke Konstruktion, leichter Lauf, Zahnsegment-Steuerung, Scheibenräder

20 cm mit dickem Gummi, Pedale verstellbar, hochwertige Lackierung, Größe 109 cm lang

Traktor zum Selbstfahren 139/3980 **73.—**

Sitzverstellung für 3 bis 6 Jahre, Stahlrohr-Rahmen, Räder mit Gummi, 15 und 24 cm

Bubirad 139/6853 **36.50** Dreirad für 2-5 Jahre, 52×63 cm, Gummipedale, leichter Lauf, Räder 10 und 20 cm

15

131

A Känguruh
4328 13.—
4350 32.50

B Zebra
6322,0 10.50
6328,0 13.80

C Cosy Orsi
6620 16.80

D Giraffe
6328,0 10.50
6335,0 14.50

E Clown
743 25.—

F Löwe
5314 10.50
5322,2 21.—

Die schönen Steiff-Tiere finden Sie in großer Auswahl bei:

759. 400. 855. Germany

Steiff
KUS 57

Margarete Steiff's
Realistic Toy Animals
(Button in Ear Brand)

LIFE-LIKE TOY ANIMALS BY MARGARETE STEIFF

We welcome you to the Steiff Zoo of stuffed animals. If you're like most people, you'll fall in love with the penguins, seals, owls, chipmunks and tigers. And you'll find represented virtually every species that stepped aboard Noah's Ark.

Today these life-like toys are collected all over the world by miniature zoo curators of all ages. The fun was started more than 75 years ago when a polio stricken girl, Margarete Steiff of Giengen on the Brenz, Germany, fashioned a stuffed elephant out of scraps of felt. It created a sensation among the children of the hamlet and Margarete's fingers flew making more elephants to give to her little friends. Soon talk of the entrancing toy spread beyond Giengen for Margarete had innocently invented the first stuffed animal in the world. When requests from neighbors were followed by orders from toy dealers, the family joined in to help Margarete, and her hobby developed into a thriving business.

As the demand grew Margarete added more animals to her miniature zoo. One of these, the Teddy Bear, first produced in the Steiff workshop, is now the most famous toy in the world.

The present generation of the Steiff family maintains old-world European standards of quality and craftsmanship. From the tiniest mouse to the largest, life-sized lion, the Steiff animals are made by hand with cherished care and affection. The furry animals are produced of the finest grade of mohair plush available, making them soft and durable. Each is imbued with a stamina required to share with a child every moment of living.

A single Steiff toy may make its first appearance in a play pen and later be found on a pillow in a college dormitory, having been companion to the same child from tot to twenties. A grandmother may hand down a Steiff toy which served as her playmate many years back.

There's a Steiff answer for the little boy who wanted to catch a squirrel and couldn't, and for the little girl who yearned to play with a seal; there's an owl to keep an insomnia victim company, a duck to comfort a disappointed hunter, a mama kangaroo (with a baby peeking brightly from her pocket) to make a busy mother smile.

Button in Ear Brand

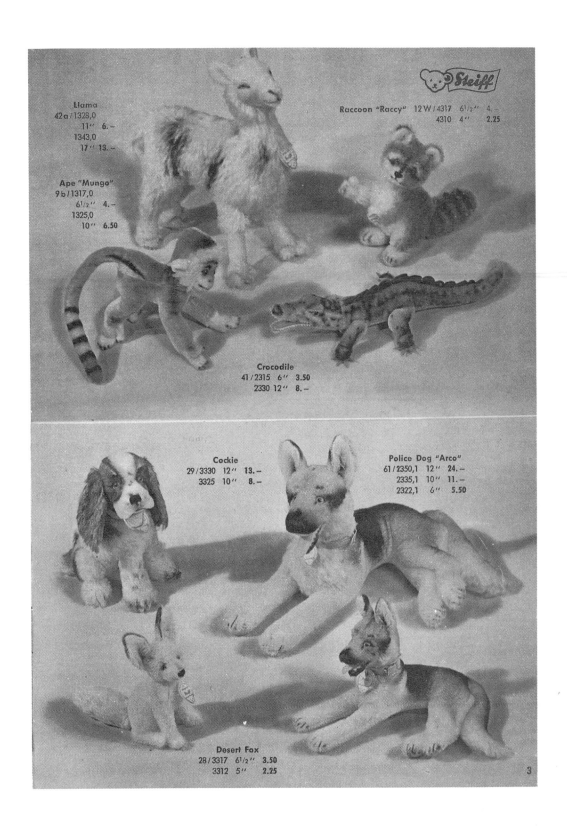

Llama
42 a / 1328,0
11" 6. –
1343,0
17" 13. –

Ape "Mungo"
9 b / 1317,0
6½" 4. –
1325,0
10" 6.50

Raccoon "Raccy" 12 W / 4317 6½" 4. –
4310 4" 2.25

Crocodile
41 / 2315 6" 3.50
2330 12" 8. –

Cockie
29 / 3330 12" 13. –
3325 10" 8. –

Police Dog "Arco"
61 / 2350,1 12" 24. –
2335,1 10" 11. –
2322,1 6" 5.50

Desert Fox
28 / 3317 6½" 3.50
3312 5" 2.25

3

Hippo
55a / 1322,0 8½" 6. –
1314,0 5" 3.50

Rhinoceros
55 / 1322,0 8½" 6. –
1314,0 5" 3.50

Leopard
48a / 1317,0 6½" 6. –
1314,0 5½" 4. –

Tiger
70 / 1317,0 6½" 6. –
1314,0 5½" 4. –

Tiger
70 / 2343,1 11" 23. –
2360,1 16" 42. –

Leopard
48a / 2343,1 11" 23. –
2360,1 16" 42. –

Tiger
70 / 2328,1
8" 10. –
2317,1
5½" 5.50

Leopard 48a / 2328,1 8" 10. –
2317,1 5½" 5.50

4

136

Steiff

King Lion "Leo"
48 /	2350,1	12"	35.—
	2335,1	10"	12.—
	2322,1	6"	7.—

Lion Cub
48 /	2343,1	11"	23.—
	2317,1	5½"	5.50
	2328,1	8"	10.—
	2360,1	16"	42.—

Leo
48/3312
5" 2.75

Lea
48/3311
4½" 2.50

Elephant
20 / 6335,0	13½"	16.—
6322,0	8½"	7.50
6317,0	6½"	5.—

Lion (jointed)
48 / 5322,2	8½"	7.50
5314	5½"	4.50

Gymnastic Ball
87 / 315	6"	3.—
320	8"	4.75
325	10"	7.50

Lion Cub
48 / 1314,0	5½"	4.—
1317,0	6½"	6.—

5

Cockie
29/1328,0   11"   11.–
       1318,0   6¹/₂"   5.–

Susi Cat
44 G/3314   5¹/₂"   3.50
       3322   8¹/₂"   5.50

Hexie
18/1313,0   5"   4.–
       1320,0   7"   6.50

Police Dog "Arco"
61/6322,0   8¹/₂"   5.–
       6317,0   6¹/₂"   4.–
       6335,0   13¹/₂"   11.–

Cockie
29/2335,1   8¹/₂"   11.–

Snobby Poodle
grey or black
58/2335,1   9"   11.–

Terry
40/1322,0   8¹/₂"   4.50
       1317,0   6¹/₂"   3.50
       1310,0   4"   1.75

Schnauzer
47/1322,0   8¹/₂"   6.–
       1314,0   5"   3.50

Joggi
37/4312   5"   2.75

Tabby Cat
44/1310,0   4"   2.–
       1314,0   5¹/₂"   3.–
       1317,0   6¹/₂"   4.–

Hamster
33/4314   5¹/₂"
       2.75

Frog
21/3410   4"   3.–
       3408   3¹/₂"   2.25

Fiffy Cat
44/2317   5"   4.–
       2325,1   7"   7.50

Steiff

Foxterrier
26/1335,02 13½'' 11.—
1322,0 8½'' 4.50
1310,0 4'' 1.75

Snobby Poodle black or grey
58/5335,2 13½'' 12.—
5314 5½'' 3.50
5322 8½'' 6.—
5343,2 17'' 20.—

Kitty Cat
44 K / 5317 6½'' 5.50
5322,2 8½'' 7.50

Turtle
65/2314 5½'' 3.—

Snobby Poodle
58/5322 8½'' 6.—

Molly Dog
68/3317 6½'' 4.75
3325,2 10'' 9.—

Bully
11/1322,02 8½'' 6.—
1317,0 6½'' 4.50

Peky
17 a/1314,0 5½'' 4.50
1322,02 8½'' 9.—
1310,0 4'' 3.—

Dally
15/3317 6½'' 4.50
3328,2 11'' 9.—

Scotty
51/1314,0 5'' 3.50
1310,0 4'' 2.—

Boxer
16/3314 5½'' 3.50
3310 4'' 2.25
1317,0 6½'' 3.50
1322,0 8½'' 4.50

7

Steiff's Miniatures
for collectors to build up an   interesting zoo

Panda	**Rhinoceros**	**Teddy**	**Hippo**	**Teddy**	**Young Bear**
12 P/1312,0 5"	55/1310,0 4"	12/5318 7" 3.—	55 a/1310,0 4"	12/5310 4" 1.50	12 a/1312,0 5"
2.50	**2.25**	5315 6" **2.25**	**2.25**	**Polar Bear**	**2.50**
				13/1312,0 5" **2.75**	

Hedgehog	**Hamster**	**Coco**	**Turtle**	**Beppo**	**Duck**	**Raccoon**
37/4312 5"	33/4310 4"	9 a/1310,0 4"	65/2310	18/5310 4"	22/6311 4"	1 2W/4310 4"
2.75	**2.—**	**2.25**	4" **2.25**	**3.50**	**1.75**	**2.25**

Kangaroo	**Lion** (jointed)	**Chimp.**	**Schnauzer**	**Bazi**	**Foxterrier**	**Hexie**
43/4314 5½"	48/5310 4"	9/5310 4"	47/1310,0 4"	18/1310,0 4"	26/1308,0 3¼"	18/1309,0 4"
2.25	**2.75**	**1.50**	**2.—**	**2.25**	**1.35**	**2.25**

Poodle	**Peky**	**Tabby Cat**	**Gussy Cat**	**Kitty Cat**	**Susi Cat**	**Bazi**
58/5310 4"	17a/1308,0 3½"	44/1307,0 3"	44/6312,0 5"	44 K/5310 4"	44 G/3310 4"	18/3310 4"
2.25	**2.25**	**1.80**	**2.25**	**3.—**	**2.25**	**2.25**

Police Dog	**Owl**	**Stork**	**Desert Fox**	**Fox**	**Raven**	**Cockie**
61/6310,0 4"	67b/4310 4"	67/1117 6½"	28/3312 5"	28/1310,0 4"	62/7312 5"	29/1311,0 4½"
2.25	**2.75**	**2.50**	**2.25**	**2.—**	**2.—**	**2.25**

8

140

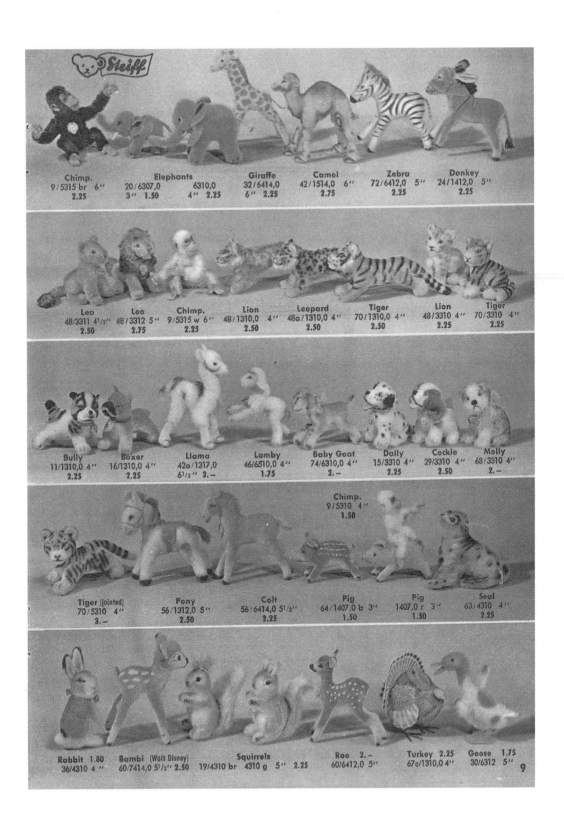

Steiff

Chimp.
9/5315 br 6"
2.25

Elephants
20/6307,0   6310,0
3" 1.50   4" 2.25

Giraffe
32/6414,0
6" 2.25

Camel
42/1514,0   6"
2.75

Zebra
72/6412,0   5"
2.25

Donkey
24/1412,0   5"
2.25

Lea
48/3311 4½"
2.50

Leo
48/3312 5"
2.75

Chimp.
9/5315 w 6"
2.25

Lion
48/1310,0   4"
2.50

Leopard
48a/1310,0   4"
2.50

Tiger
70/1310,0   4"
2.50

Lion
48/3310 4"
2.25

Tiger
70/3310 4"
2.25

Bully
11/1310,0 4"
2.25

Boxer
16/1310,0 4"
2.25

Llama
42a/1317,0
6½" 3.—

Lamby
46/6510,0 4"
1.75

Baby Goat
74/6310,0 4"
2.—

Dally
15/3310 4"
2.25

Cockie
29/3310 4"
2.50

Molly
68/3310 4"
2.—

Chimp.
9/5310   4"
1.50

Tiger (jointed)
70/5310 4"
3.—

Pony
56/1312,0 5"
2.50

Colt
56/6414,0 5½"
2.25

Pig
64/1407,0 b 3"
1.50

Pig
1407,0 r 3"
1.50

Seal
63/4310 4"
2.25

Rabbit 1.80
36/4310 4"

Bambi (Walt Disney)
60/7414,0 5½" 2.50

Squirrels
19/4310 br   4310 g 5" 2.25

Roe 2.—
60/6412,0 5"

Turkey 2.25
67a/1310,0 4"

Goose 1.75
30/6312 5"

9

Teddy
12/5350,2	20''	15.—
5365,2	25¹/₂''	29.—
5375,2	29¹/₂''	45.—
5343,2	17''	12.—

Chimpanzee
9/5335	13¹/₂''	7.—
5350,2	20''	15.—
5360,2	23¹/₂''	21.—
5380,2	31¹/₂''	39.50
5325	10''	4.50

Steiff

Coco
9a/1322,0	8¹/₂''	5.—
1314,0	5¹/₂''	3.50

Zotty
12Z/6343,2	17''	15.—
6350,2	20''	20.—

Original Teddy   Koala

12/5322,2	5325,2	5328,2	5335,2	5340,2	12K/4312	5322	5335,2
8¹/₂'' 3.50	10'' 4.—	11'' 5.—	13¹/₂'' 6.50	16'' 9.—	5'' 2.75	8¹/₂'' 5.50	13¹/₂'' 11.—

Zotty

10	12Z/6317,1	6322,1	6335,1 13¹/₂'' 11.—	6343,2 17'' 15.—
	6¹/₂'' 4.—	8¹/₂'' 5.—	6328,1 11'' 7.50	6350,2 20'' 20.—

Cosy Wash Animals of DRALON Plush filled with foam rubber, fully washable

Cosy Teddy	Cosy Teddy	Cosy Orsi	Cosy Elephant
83/12/5622 8'' **6.—**	12/5630 12'' **6.50**	12/6620 8'' **6.—**	20/6620 8'' **6.—**

Cosy Molly	Cosy Kitty	Cosy Mummy	Cosy Raccy (Raccoon)
68/6620 8'' **6.—**	44/6620 8'' **6.—**	36/6620 8'' **6.—**	12w/6620 8'' **6.50**

Floppy Sleeping Animals
Very soft and cuddly

Floppy Panda
85/12P/7328 6'' 6.—
7317 5'' 3.—

Floppy Bear
85/12/7328 6'' 6.—

12/7317 5'' 3.—

Floppy Rabbit
85/36/7328 6'' 6.—
7317 5'' 3.—

Floppy Cockie	Floppy Cat	Floppy Lamb	Floppy Tiger
85/29/7328 6'' 6.—	44/7328 6'' 6.—	46/7528 6'' 6.—	70/7328 6'' 6.—
7317 5'' 3.—	7317 5'' 3.—	7517 5'' 3.—	7317 5'' 3.—

11

Hand Puppets

Hand Squirrel
79/19/317 6" 3.25

Hand Cockie
29/317 6" 3.75

Hand Santa Claus
79/88/121
11" 4.75

Crocodile
41/317
6" 3.75

Lion
48/317
6" 3.25

Fox
28/317
6" 3.25

Owl
67 B/317
6" 3.25

Hand Teddy
79/12/317 6" 3.25

Wolf
61a/317 6" 3.25

Rabbit
36/317 6" 3.25

Bully
11/317 6" 3.25

Poodle
58/317 6" 3.25

Hand Boxer
79/16/317 6" 3.25

Hand Foxy
26/317 6" 3.25

Cat
44/317 6" 3.25

Tom Cat
44/717 6" 3.25

Molly
68/317 6" 3.25

12

Hand Puppets

Hand Chimpanzee
79/9/317 6″ 3.25

Hand Tiger
79/70/317 6″ 3.25

Wool Miniatures

Mouse

Chipmunk

50/2504,2 1½″ −.80   2504,1 1½″ −.80   45/2506 2½″ 1.− **Skunk**   19/4505 2″ 1.−   **Cat** 44/3505 2″ 1.−

Cheerup Birds
4 colors − 4 types
5/1509, 1-4 3½″ −.90

Snobby Poodle
58/1506 2½″ 1.−

Ladybird
39/1503 1¼″ −.35
1504 1¾″ −.50

Birds 5 colors − 5 types
5/6504,1−5 1½″ −.50
6508,1−5 3¼″ −.80

Rabbits
36/2504,1−5 1½″ −.80
2506,1−5 2½″ 1.25

22/1506 b 2½″ −.90 **Ducks** 1504 1½″ −.50 1506 g 2½″ −.90

Cock 34/1508
3½″ −.90

Hen 35/1508
3½″ −.90

Chicken 35/1504 1½″ −.50
1506 2½″ −.80

Raven 62/1308
3¼″ −.90

Pigeon
8/1506 2½″ −.90

13

Steiff

Deer 60/1335,0 13½'' 7.—

Roe 60/1328,0 11'' 6.—

Squirrels brown or grey

Fawn
60/6322,0 8½'' 4.—
6317,0 6½'' 3.50
6314,0 5½'' 2.50

19/4322 8½'' 5.—

19/4314 5½'' 3.50

Persian Lamb

Horse 56/1328,0 11'' 7.—
1322,0 8½'' 4.75

Jumbo 20/4322,1 8½'' 6.75

Donkey
24/1322,0 8½'' 5.50
1328,0 11'' 7.—

46a/6322,0 8½'' 6.—
6328,0 11'' 9.50
6335,0 13½'' 13.—

Owl

Turkey
67a/1314,0
5½'' 3.50

Niki Rabbit
36/5322 8½'' 4.75
5317 6½'' 3.75

Lulac
36/7343,1 17'' 7.—

67b/4322 8½'' 7.—
4314 5'' 3.50

14

Reindeer
60 a / 1322,0   8¹/₂″   5.50
      1314,0   5¹/₂″   3.—

Penguin
54 / 4322   8¹/₂″   4.—
     4310   4″   2.—
     4314   5¹/₂″   2.50
     4335   13¹/₂″   6.50

Polar Bear
13 / 1317,02   6¹/₂″   4.50
      1325,02   10″   7.—

Seal
63 / 4314   5″   **3.50**
     4310   4″   **2.25**

Camel
42 / 1528,0   11″   **5.50**
      1535,0   13¹/₂″   **7.50**

Giraffe
32 / 6335,0   13¹/₂″   **5.50**
      6328,0   11″   **4.—**
      6350,0   20″   **11.—**

Young Bear
12 a / 1317,02   6¹/₂″   4.—
      1325,02   10″   8.50

Zebra
72 / 6322,0   8¹/₂″   4.—
      6328,0   11″   5.—
      6335,0   13¹/₂″   7.50

15

147

TV Animals

Snuggy Slo (Turtle)
82/65/2343 17" 35.—

Snuggy Jumbo (Elephant)
82/20/7355,0 22" 39.50

Kangaroo
43/4350 20" 14.—
4328 11" 4.75

Steiff

KUS 59

Margarete Steiff's
Realistic Plush Animals
(Button in Ear Brand)

Every moment, in every nation of the world, a Steiff toy is part of the life of some little boy or girl. One may be found in the arms of a sleeping child or several may decorate a nursery. A Steiff lion or Teddy Bear may be companion to a little boy on his flights into fancy. A little girl may be seen placing a loving kiss on the soft cheek of her Steiff lamb or kitten.

A Steiff toy will share a child's busy day and listen patiently to its joys and sorrows. It will withstand ferocious hugging and furious play, yet when bedtime comes, it is ready to sleep quietly beside its daytime playmate providing the assurance of a friend close by.

Steiff toys are made in much the same way they were more than 75 years ago when the deep love a kindly seamstress had for children prompted her to produce the world's first stuffed toy. The same high standards of craftmanship and quality first set down by Margarete Steiff in the year 1880 are still maintained today. Though thousands of toys leave daily from the quaint German hamlet of Giengen on the Brenz where the Steiff factory is located, each has been individually created in the gentle hands of a skilled toymaker.

The individual handcrafting of Steiff animals produces slight variations in facial expression, giving each a personality of its own. Thus some may appear to be pondering a deep thought while others may seem on the verge of a mischievous gambol or smiling a gentle puppy-dog smile. All, though, bear the characteristic, very special charm that unmistakeably identifies a Steiff toy. Steiff is now the world's largest producer of stuffed animals. A variety of more than 600 toys, representing practically every member of the animal kingdom, is contained in the Steiff zoo and their appeal is universal. Collectors in every corner of the globe are filling their shelves with miniature Steiff trophies. Teen-agers are using them as top of bed decorations or „gab session" companions and owners of earlier Steiff toys are handing them down as heirlooms. Steiff toys are placed at the top of gift lists as appropriate for just about any occasion.

Steiff toys are made of the finest obtainable grade of mohair plush unless otherwise indicated. Where size permits, all are equipped with voices. Each Steiff toy carries the world-famous trademark

Button in Ear

All animals are, if no other indication, of finest glossy mohair plush.
All animals have voices if size of body has space enough.

Novelties 1959

Walrus "Paddy"
631/4310,00 4"   3.—
4314,00 5¹/₂" 4.50
4322,00 8¹/₂" 7.50

Pelican "Piccy"
545/1317,00 6¹/₂" 4.—
1325,00 10" 6.75

Sea horse "Sigi"
830/665/4620,00 7¹/₂" 5.50
4628,00 11" 8.—

Cocker Spaniel "Revue Susi"
290/3312,03 5"   3.—
3317,03 6¹/₂" 5.50
3328,03 11" 10.—

Badger "Diggy"
185/4310,00 4" 2.25
4315,00 6" 3.50

Perri
(Cop. W. Disney)
191/4312,03 5" 2.75
4317,03 6¹/₂" 4.—

Lizard "Lizzy"
195/1404,00 1¹/₂" 2.25
1406,00 2¹/₂" 3.50

Tapsy Cat
440/1308,00 3¹/₄" 2.—
1311,00 4¹/₂" 2.75
1315,00 6" 3.50
1318,00 7" 5.—

Cosy Siamy Cat
830/440/7617,00
6¹/₂" 3.50

Floppy Beagle
850/230/7317,00
6¹/₂" 3.50

Floppy Poodle white
850/580/7317,04 6¹/₂" 3.50
7328,04 11" 6.75

Finch
622/6310,03
4" 4.—

Birds
Bluebonnet
6310,04 4" 4.—

Bullfinch
6310,06 4" 4.—

Miniature Poodle
581/1325,06 10" 8.—
1330,06 12" 12.—

Tiger
700/3314,00 5¹/₂" 4.—
3322,00 8¹/₂" 7.50
3343,00 17" 22.—

Frog
310/3328,00 11" 11.—

Mountain Lamb
462/1312,00 5" 2.50
1317,00 6¹/₂" 3.50
1322,00 8¹/₂" 6.—

3

Steiff

Chimpanzee "Jocko"

090/5325,03			Monkey "Mungo"		
10"	**5.—**		102/1317,07	7½"	**4.—**
5335,03	13½"	**7.50**	1325,07	10"	**6.75**
5350,03	20"	**17.—**	1335,07	13½"	**12.50**
5360,03	23½"	**24.—**			
5380,03	31½"	**42.50**			

Original Teddy

gold ,01, caramel ,02 darkbrown ,03 or white ,04
120/5322,01—04
8½" **3.75**
5328,01—04 11" **5.50**
5335,01—04 13½" **6.75**
5340,01—04 16" **10.—**

Zotty Bear

121/6317,00			6322,00	8½"	**5.50**
6½"	**4.—**		6328,00	11"	**8.—**
			6335,00	13½"	**11.50**

Snobby Poodle, jointed
white ,04 or grey ,05 or black ,06

580/5914,04—06	5322,04—06	5335,04—06	5343,04—06
5½" **3.50**	8½" **6.—**	13½" **12.50**	17" **18.50**

King Lion "Leo"

4 480/2322,00 6" **7.—**   2335,00 10" **12.50**   2350,00 12" **35.—**

Tiger
700/2317,00 5¹/₂ 5.50
2328,00 8" 10.—
2343,00 11" 23.—
2360,00 16" 42.—

King Lion "Leo"
480/2350,00 12" 35.—

Pelican "Piccy"
545/1317,00 6¹/₂" 4.—
1325,00 10" 6.75

Monkey "Mungo"
102/1317,07 7¹/₂" 4.—
1325,07 10" 6.75
1335,07 13¹/₂" 12.50

Kangaroo
430/4314,00 5¹/₂" 2.75
4328,00 11" 5.50
4350,00 20" 15.—
4365,00 25¹/₂" 24.—

Llama
425/1317,00 6¹/₂" 3.25
1328,00 11" 6.—
1343,00 17" 14.—

Penguin "Peggy"
540/4314,07 5¹/₂" 2.50
4322,07 8¹/₂" 4.—
4335,07 13¹/₂" 7.—
4350,07 20" 16.—

Raccoon "Raccy"
126/4310,00 4" 2.25
4317,00 6¹/₂" 4.—

5

Basset "Hexie"

180/1309,00	4''	2.50
1313,00	5''	4.50
1320,00	7''	6.75
1325,00	10''	11.—

Cocker Spaniel "Cockie"

290/1318,00		1328,00	
6¹/₂''	5.—	11''	11.—

Cocker Spaniel "Cockie"

290/3314,00		3325,00	10''	8.—
5¹/₂''	4.—	3330,00	12''	12.50

Beagle Dog "Biggie"

230/1317,00	6¹/₂''	4.50
1325,00	10''	8.—

Foxterrier

260/1308,00	3¹/₄''	1.50	1322,00	8¹/₂''	4.75
1310,00	4''	1.75	1328,00	11''	6.75
1317,00	6¹/₂''	4.—	1335,00	13¹/₂''	10.50

Pekinese

172/1308,00	3¹/₂''	2.25	1314,00	5¹/₂''	5.—
1310,00	4''	3.25	1322,00	8¹/₂''	9.—

6

470/1310,00			1322,00	8¹/₂''	6.75
4''	2.25		1328,00	11''	9.—

Snauzer "Tessie"

	1314,00	5''	3.50

Bully

110/1317,00	6¹/₂''	5.—
1322,00	8¹/₂''	6.50

Steiff

Beagle Dog
230/1325,00
10″ 8.—

Poodle
grey ,05 black ,06
580/2335,05—06
9″ 11.50

Tapsy Cat
440/1318,00
7″ 5.—

Pekinese
172/1314,00
5¹/₂″ 5.—

Poodle, white ,04 grey ,05 or black ,06
580/5322,04—06 8¹/₂″ 6.—

Owl "Wittie"
674/4314,00 5″ 3.50
4322,00 8¹/₂″ 7.—

Perri (Cop. W. Disney)
191/4317,03 6¹/₂″ 4.—

Turtle "Slo"
650/2322,00
8¹/₂″ 7.—

Frog "Froggy"
310/3410,00
4″ 3.25

Beaver "Nagy"
194/4317,00
6¹/₂″ 4.—

Lizard "Lizzy"
195/1404,00 1¹/₂″ 2.25
1406,00 2¹/₂″ 3.50

7

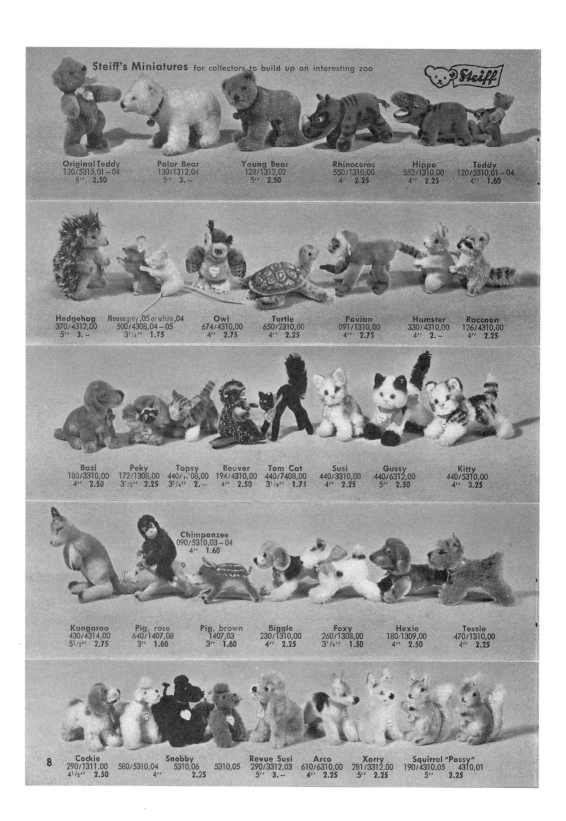

Steiff's Miniatures for collectors to build up an interesting zoo

Steiff

Original Teddy	**Polar Bear**	**Young Bear**	**Rhinoceros**	**Hippo**	**Teddy**
120/5315,01 – 04	130/1312,04	128/1312,02	550/1310,00	552/1310,00	120/5310,01 – 04
6″ **2.50**	5″ **3.–**	5″ **2.50**	4″ **2.25**	4″ **2.25**	4″ **1.60**

Hedgehog	**Mouse** grey ,05 or white ,04	**Owl**	**Turtle**	**Pavian**	**Hamster**	**Raccoon**
370/4312,00	500/4308,04 – 05	674/4310,00	650/2310,00	091/1310,00	330/4310,00	126/4310,00
5″ **3.–**	3¼″ **1.75**	4″ **2.75**	4″ **2.25**	4″ **2.75**	4″ **2.–**	4″ **2.25**

Bazi	**Peky**	**Tapsy**	**Beaver**	**Tom Cat**	**Susi**	**Gussy**	**Kitty**
180/3310,00	172/1308,00	440/1308,00	194/4310,00	440/7408,00	440/3310,00	440/6312,00	440/5310,00
4″ **2.50**	3½″ **2.25**	3¼″ **2.–**	4″ **2.50**	3¼″ **1.75**	4″ **2.25**	5″ **2.50**	4″ **3.25**

Chimpanzee
090/5310,03 – 04
4″ **1.60**

Kangaroo	**Pig, rose**	**Pig, brown**	**Biggle**	**Foxy**	**Hexie**	**Tessie**
430/4314,00	640/1407,08	1407,03	230/1310,00	260/1308,00	180/1309,00	470/1310,00
5½″ **2.75**	3″ **1.60**	3″ **1.60**	4″ **2.25**	3¼″ **1.50**	4″ **2.50**	4″ **2.25**

8

Cockie	**Snobby**			**Revue Susi**	**Arco**	**Xorry**	**Squirrel "Possy"**
290/1311,00	580/5310,04	5310,06	5310,05	290/3312,03	610/6310,00	281/3312,00	190/4310,05 4310,01
4½″ **2.50**	4″	**2.25**		5″ **3.–**	4″ **2.25**	5″ **2.25**	5″ **2.25**

156

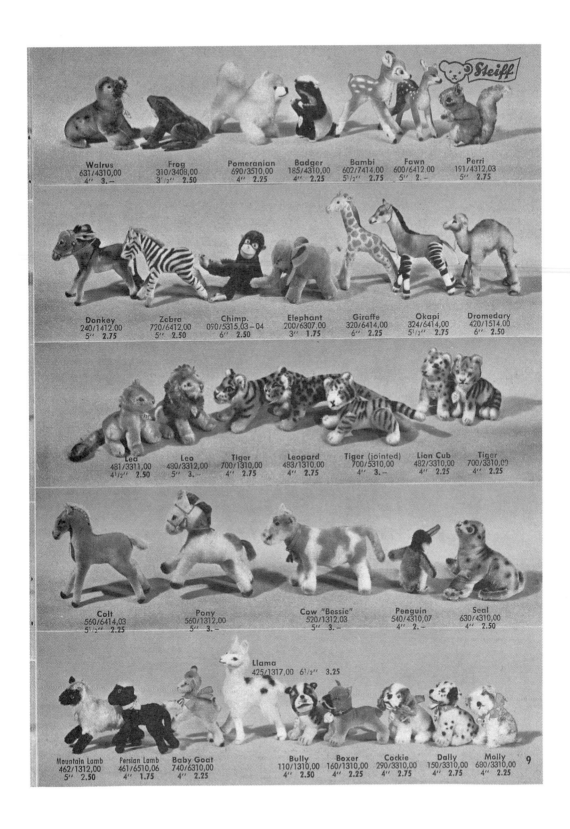

Walrus	Frog	Pomeranian	Badger	Bambi	Fawn	Perri
631/4310,00	310/3408,00	690/3510,00	185/4310,00	602/7414,00	600/6412,00	191/4312,03
4" 3.—	3½" 2.50	4" 2.25	4" 2.25	5½" 2.75	5" 2.—	5" 2.75

Donkey	Zebra	Chimp.	Elephant	Giraffe	Okapi	Dromedary
240/1412,00	720/6412,00	090/5315,03–04	200/6307,00	320/6414,00	324/6414,00	420/1514,00
5" 2.75	5" 2.50	6" 2.50	3" 1.75	6" 2.25	5½" 2.75	6" 2.50

Lea	Leo	Tiger	Leopard	Tiger (jointed)	Lion Cub	Tiger
481/3311,00	480/3312,00	700/1310,00	483/1310,00	700/5310,00	482/3310,00	700/3310,00
4½" 2.50	5" 3.—	4" 2.75	4" 2.75	4" 3.—	4" 2.25	4" 2.25

Colt	Pony	Cow "Bessie"	Penguin	Seal
560/6414,03	560/1312,00	520/1312,03	540/4310,07	630/4310,00
5½" 2.25	5" 3.—	5" 3.—	4" 2.—	4" 2.50

Llama
425/1317,00 6½" 3.25

Mountain Lamb	Persian Lamb	Baby Goat	Bully	Boxer	Cockie	Dally	Molly
462/1312,00	461/6510,06	740/6310,00	110/1310,00	160/1310,00	290/3310,00	150/3310,00	680/3310,00
5" 2.50	4" 1.75	4" 2.25	4" 2.50	4" 2.25	4" 2.75	4" 2.75	4" 2.25

9

Steiff

Desert Fox			Frog			Mickl (Cop. Diehl Film)		Meckl		Beaver			Squirrel		
281/3312,00	5''	2.25	310/3410,00			900/8717,80	6½'' 4.–	8717,70		194/4310,00	4''	2.50	190/4310,05	4''	2.25
3317,00	6½''	3.50		4''	3.25	8728,80	11'' 7.–	8728,70		4317,00	6½''	4.–	4314,05	5½''	3.50
													4322,05	8½''	5.25

Lion Cub			Lion "Leo" (jointed)			Leopard		
482/2317,00	5½''	5.50	480/5314,00	5½''	4.75	483/2317,00	5½''	5.50
2328,00	8''	10.–	5322,00	8½''	7.50	2328,00	8''	10.–
2343,00	11''	23.–				2343,00	11''	23.–
2360,00	16''	42.–				2360,00	16''	42.–

Jumbo			Reindeer			Donkey			Hippo			Rhinoceros		
200/4322,00	8½''	6.75	603/1314,00	5½''	3.–	240/1314,00	5''	4.–	552/1310,00	4''	2.25	550/1310,00	4''	2.25
4335,00	13½''	17.–	1322,00	8½''	5.50	1322,00	8½''	5.50	1314,00	5''	3.50	1314,00	5''	3.50
						1328,00	11''	7.50	1322,00	8½''	6.–	1322,00	8½''	6.–

10

Tiger			Polar Dog			Hedgehog			Molly (Young Dog)		
700/1310,00	4''	2.75	695/1317,00	6½''	4.50	370/4312,00			680/3310,00	4''	2.25
1314,00	5½''	4.–	1325,00	10''	8.50		5''	3.–	3317,00	6½''	5.25
1317,00	6½''	6.–							3325,00	10''	9.–

Deer	**Roe**	**Bambf** (cop. W. Disney)	**Dwarfs** Lucki: ,02 Puckl: ,03		**Cow "Bessy"**
600/1335,00	1328,00	602/7414,00 5¹/₂" **2.75**	901/8713,02 – 03 5" **2.50**		520/1317,03 6¹/₂" **5.–**
13¹/₂" **7.–**	11" **6.50**	7422,00 8¹/₂" **4.50**	8718,02 – 03 7¹/₂" **4.75**		1325,03 10" **7.50**
			8730,02 – 03 12" **8.50**		
			8755,02 – 03 22" **25.–**		

Poodle "Snobby"
grey ,05 or black ,06
580/2335,05 – 06 9" **11.50**

Cocker Spaniel "Cockie"
290/2335,06 8¹/₂" **12.–**

Police Dog "Arco"
610/2322,00 6" **5.50**
2335,00 10" **11.–**
2350,00 12" **25.–**

Boxer	**Fiffy Cat**	**Susi Cat**	**Boxer**	**Tabby Cat**
160/3310,00 4" **2.25**	440/2317,00 5" **4.–**	440/3314,00 5¹/₂" **3.50**	160/1317,00 6¹/₂" **3.50**	440/1307,00 3" **2.–**
3314,00 5¹/₂" **4.–**	2325,00 7" **7.50**	3322,00 8¹/₂" **6.–**	1322,00 8¹/₂" **5.–**	1310,00 4" **2.25**
				1314,00 5¹/₂" **3.25**
				1317,00 6¹/₂" **4.–**

Horse   **Dwarf "Gucki"**   **Tom Cat**   **Kitty Cat**   **Arco**   **Dally**

560/1322,04 8¹/₂" **5.25**	901/8713,01 5" **2.50**	440/7410,00	5310,00 4" **3.25**	610/6310,00 4" **2.25**	150/3317,00
1328,04 11" **7.–**	8718,01 7¹/₂" **4.75**	4" **2.25**	5317,00 6¹/₂" **6.–**	6317,00 6¹/₂" **4.–**	6¹/₂" **5.–**
1335,04 13¹/₂" **11.–**	8730,01 12" **8.50**		5322,00 8¹/₂" **8.–**	6322,00 8¹/₂" **5.25**	3328,00
	8755,01 22" **25.–**			6335,00 13¹/₂" **11.–**	11" **10.–**

11

159

Hand Puppets

Steiff

Hand Chimpanzee	Mungo	Leo	Crocodile	Cockie
865/090/0317,00	102/0318,00	480/0318,00	410/0317,00	290/0317,00
6" **3.25**	6" **3.75**	6" **3.75**	6" **3.75**	6" **3.75**

Hand Teddy	Fox	Wolf	Rabbit	Poodle
865/120/0317,00	280/0317,00	612/0317,00	360/0317,00	580/0317,00
6" **3.25**	6" **3.25**	6" **3.75**	6" **3.25**	6" **3.75**

Hand Squirrel	Owl	Lioness	Tiger	Bully
865/190/0317.01–05	674/0317,00	481/0317,00	700/0317,00	110/0317,00
6" **3.25**	6" **3.25**	6" **3.25**	6" **3.25**	6" **3.25**

Hand Tom Cat	Cat	Boxer	Molly	Foxy
865/440/0717,00	440/0317,00	160/0317,00	680/0317,00	260/0317,00
6" **3.25**	6" **3.25**	6" **3.25**	6" **3.25**	6" **3.25**

12

Mimic Animals – perfect animation. All 5 fingers enable you to manipulate head, mouth and paws together and separately. Also Floppy Sleeping Animals with pillow inside.

Steiff

Mimic Biggie
866/230/0328,00 6" **7.–**

Mimic Tessie
470/0328,00 6" **7.–**

Mimic Dally
150/0328,00 6" **7.–**

Wool-Miniatures

Mouse
886/2504,45 1¹⁄₂" **–.85**
2504,44 1¹⁄₂" **–.85**

Skunk
890/2506,40
2¹⁄₂" **1.–**

Chipmunk
876/4505,43
2" **1.–**

Cat
884/3505,40
2" **–.95**

Cheerup Birds
4 colors - 4 types
873/1509 3¹⁄₂" **–.85**

Snobby Poodle
894/1506
2¹⁄₂" **1.–**

Ladybird
880/1503,40 1¹⁄₄" **–.35**
1504,40 1³⁄₄" **–.50**

Birds
5 colors – 5 types
871/6504 2¹⁄₂" **–.50**
6508 3¹⁄₄" **–.75**

Rabbits
2 sizes – 5 colors
875/2504 1¹⁄₂" **–.90**
2506 2¹⁄₂" **1.25**

Ducks
877/1506,47
2¹⁄₂" **–.90**
1504,41 1¹⁄₂" **–.50**
1506,41 2¹⁄₂" **–.85**

Cock 878/1508,47
3¹⁄₂" **–.95**

Hen 879/1508,44
3¹⁄₄" **–.95**

Chicken
879/1504,41 1¹⁄₂" **–.50**
1506,41 2¹⁄₂" **–.75**

Raven
888/1508,46
3¹⁄₄" **–.95**

Pigeon
892/1506,40
2¹⁄₂" **–.85**

13

Steiff

Elephant

Koala Bear

124/5312,00	5''	3.–
5322,00	8½''	6.–
5335,00	13½''	12.–

200/6310,00	4''	**2.25**
6317,00	6½''	**5.50**
6322,00	8½''	**7.50**
6335,00	13½''	**17.–**

Clownie

902/8714,00	5½''	**2.50**
8719,00	8½''	**4.75**
8743,00	17''	**12.–**

Giraffe

320/6328,00	11''	**4.–**
6335,00	13½''	**5.50**
6350,00	20''	**11.50**

Okapi

324/6428,00	11''	**5.25**
6443,00	17''	**11.–**

Ball

855/7315,07	6''	**3.–**
7320,07	8''	**5.–**
7325,07	10''	**8.–**

Cosy Xorry (Fox)
830/280/7617,00   5'' **3.50**

Cosy Foxy (Foxterrier)
260/7617,00   5'' **3.50**

Turtle "Slo"
650/2322,00   8½'' **7.–**

Cosy Wash Animals

DRALON (e.Wz.) plush, filled with
foam rubber, fully washable

Cosy Teddy
830/120/5622,00
8'' **6.–**

Cosy Teddy
120/5630,00
12'' **6.75**

Cosy Orsi
128/6620,00
8'' **6.–**

Cosy Elephant
200/6620,00
8'' **6.–**

Cosy Mummy

Cosy Raccy (Raccoon)

Cosy Kitty

Cosy Molly

14

830/360/6620,00 8'' **6.–**

126/6620,00 8'' **6.75**

440/6620,00 8'' **6.–**

680/6620,00 8'' **6.–**

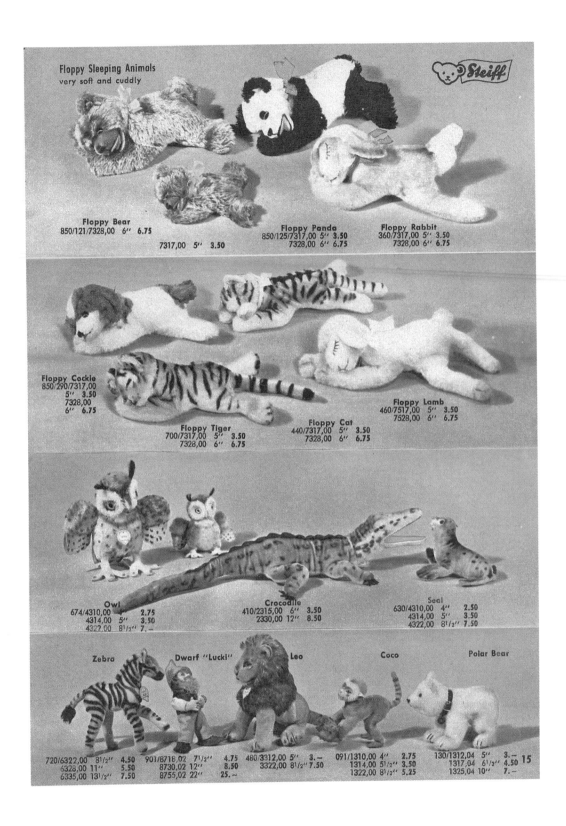

Floppy Sleeping Animals
very soft and cuddly

Steiff

Floppy Bear
850/121/7328,00 6" **6.75**
7317,00 5" **3.50**

Floppy Panda
850/125/7317,00 5" **3.50**
7328,00 6" **6.75**

Floppy Rabbit
360/7317,00 5" **3.50**
7328,00 6" **6.75**

Floppy Cockie
850/290/7317,00
5" **3.50**
7328,00
6" **6.75**

Floppy Tiger
700/7317,00 5" **3.50**
7328,00 6" **6.75**

Floppy Cat
440/7317,00 5" **3.50**
7328,00 6" **6.75**

Floppy Lamb
460/7517,00 5" **3.50**
7528,00 6" **6.75**

Owl
674/4310,00 4" **2.75**
4314,00 5" **3.50**
4322,00 8¹/₂" **7.—**

Crocodile
410/2315,00 6" **3.50**
2330,00 12" **8.50**

Seal
630/4310,00 4" **2.50**
4314,00 5" **3.50**
4322,00 8¹/₂" **7.50**

Zebra
720/6322,00 8¹/₂" **4.50**
6328,00 11" **5.50**
6335,00 13¹/₂" **7.50**

Dwarf "Lucki"
901/8718,02 7¹/₂" **4.75**
8730,02 12" **8.50**
8755,02 22" **25.—**

Leo
480/3312,00 5" **3.—**
3322,00 8¹/₂" **7.50**

Coco
091/1310,00 4" **2.75**
1314,00 5¹/₂" **3.50**
1322,00 8¹/₂" **5.25**

Polar Bear
130/1312,04 5" **3.—**
1317,04 6¹/₂" **4.50**
1325,04 10" **7.—**

15

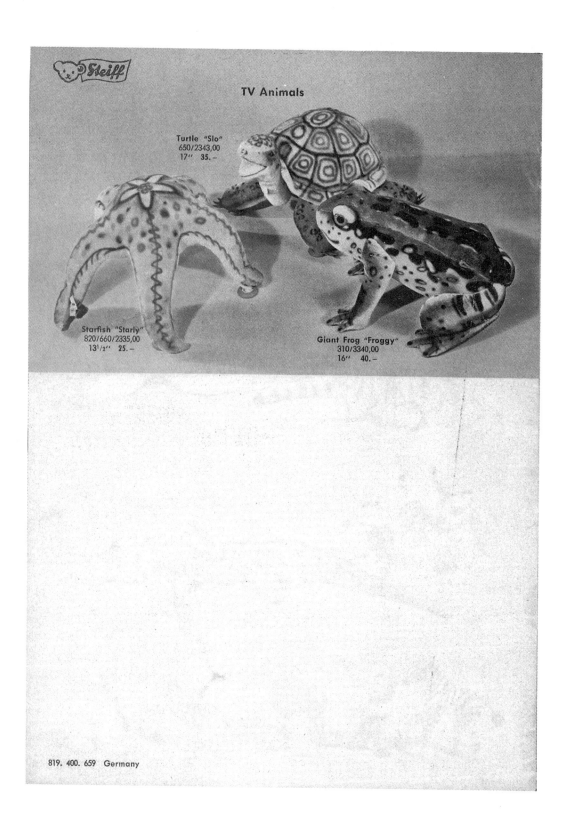

TV Animals

Turtle "Slo"
650/2343,00
17"   35.—

Starfish "Starly"
820/660/2335,00
13¹/₂"   25.—

Giant Frog "Froggy"
310/3340,00
16"   40.—

1960's

The
Steiff-Zoo

lifelike stuffed toys by
MARGARETE STEIFF

Perri
(Cop. Walt Disney)

Molly Dog
Just a Pet

Steiff

look for the Button-in-Ear

The friendliest Zoo

The large assortment of stuffed toy animals from the workshops of the Margarete Steiff toy factory comprise the world's biggest and friendliest zoo collection.

Known throughout the world for their beauty and charm, Steiff toys are made in much the same manner as they were more than eighty years ago when the company first opened its doors. The same high standards of quality set then by Margarete Steiff, the kindly seamstress who was the company's founder, are rigidly adhered to today.

All Steiff toys are still made carefully and lovingly by hand of the best materials that are obtainable. The finest detail is painstakingly carried out to see that each toy has the color, shape and marking of the animal it represents. The tradition established by Margarete Steiff gives each the delightful qualities of warmth and charm that no other company has been able to equal.

Steiff toys range from one inch miniatures to full life size. All are extremely suitable for private zoo collections, or just plain cuddling.

Steiff

look for the Button in the Ear

Biggie The Beagle

Biggie the Beagle is a mild mannered hound
his bark's called a bugle, his manner profound.

Zotty
The Shaggy Bear

ZOTTY, dear Zotty is a special type bear
he smiles and he grumbles and has the shaggiest hair.

Longneck
The Giraffe
The GIRAFFE is a tall one, in fact he's taller than all,
From his head to the ground is a mighty big fall.

Trampy
The jolly Elephant
TRAMPY'S an elephant, a baby at that.
He's roly and poly and awfully fat.

Snucki The Mountain Ram
SNUCKI the Mountain Goat is most regal they say.
He charges and butts, but only in play.

Mecki (Cop. Diehl Films)
The Hedgehog-Papa

This kindly old hedgehog is called MECKI by name.
He has a wife and two children, and they look quite the same.

Leo
King of the animals

LEO the Lion, as everyone knows,
is King of the beasts from his head to his toes.

Steiff

The good old
Original Teddy

The illustrious TEDDY BEAR was first made by Steiff
he's the most lovable toy you'll meet in this life.

Xorry
The Desert Fox

XORRY is a desert fox who spells
his name confusingly,
he looks like a puppy dog and does
it most amusingly.

Orsi
The Bear Cub

ORSI the Bear Cub is Teddy's true friend.
He's polite and he's pleasant and he'll never offend.

Lucki
The smiling Dwarf
LUCKI the dwarf is one
of three brothers
Gucki and Pucki
are the names
of the others.

Lulac
The happy Hare
LULAC the Rabbit is a superior
clown.
You can hug him and squeeze him
or turn him upside down.

Froggy
The jumper

It is natural indeed to call this frog, FROGGY,
but can you imagine anyone calling a polliwog, Polliwoggy?

Okapi
stately and serious

The stately OKAPI is rare and mysterious
He's from the dark continent and his manner's mostly serious.

Steiff

Raccy
the playful Raccoon

The RACCOON is a playful pet whose appearance is deceiving
Although he wears an outlaw's mask, his business isn't thieving.

Llama
the wooly one

The LLAMA is a beast
of burden who comes
from the Andes
He'll eat almost any-
thing including cakes
and candies.

Peggy
the pert Penguin

PEGGY the Penguin has
a funny way of walking
She waddles and wigg-
les and you should hear
her talking.

Snobby
the perky Poodle

SNOBBY the Poodle is perky and quite prim
SNOBBY's not her real name, it's just a pseudonym.

Jocko
the Chimpanzee

JOCKO is a monkey, a playful, prankful imp
Jester of the jungle, he's more often called a Chimp.

Slo
the Turtle

SLO is a Turtle most steady in his ways
He wears his house upon his back and never disobeys.

Buck
the male Deer

The BUCK is a male Deer who
wears antlers on his head
Wonder what he does with them
when it's time to go to bed.

Nagy
The busy Beaver

NAGY is a busy Beaver, busy all the day
Busy as he always is, he still finds time for play.

Bambi
Cop. Walt Disney

BAMBI is a bright-eyed fawn whose ways are most
endearing
He's very nice to have around on days when you
need cheering.

Leo
The brave Lion

The Lion is the king
of beasts, his title's
most befitting
You saw him lying
down before, now you
see him sitting.

Mungo
the jungle mischief-maker
MUNGO is a ring-tailed monkey with mischief on his
mind
His tricks and pranks are all in play and he's very, very
kind.

821. 200 160 Germany